50 LIFE-BUILDING STORIES

By the same author

50 Stories for Special Occasions
50 Five-Minute Stories
The Brownie Guide Book
Love Breaks Through
Jessica Joins the Brownies
Tracy and the Warriors
A Friend for Life
Failure is Never Final

50 Life-Building Stories

LYNDA NEILANDS

EASTBOURNE

To Mum and Dad

Contents

Acknowledgements   10
Introduction   11

Part One: CONSCIENCE-BUILDING STORIES
The Castle - A story series introducing the Ten
*   Commandments*
 1 Laws for Living   15
 2 The Blue Pencil *(No other gods before me)*   21
 3 The Red Pencil *(No idols)*   28
 4 The Black Pencil *(Respect God's name)*   34
 5 The Yellow Pencil *(Remember the Sabbath)*   39
 6 The Green Pencil *(Honour your parents)*   45
 7 The Brown Pencil *(No killing)*   50
 8 The Orange Pencil *(Be faithful in marriage)*   56
 9 The Purple Pencil *(No stealing)*   62
10 The Grey Pencil *(No lying)*   67
11 The White Pencil *(No coveting)*   74
12 The Crown of Gold   81
13 From Jonathan's Diary   89

Part Two: CHARACTER-BUILDING STORIES

Rhyming stories on the wisdom of Proverbs

14 King Solomon's Dream *(Put God first)*   97
15 Bert and the Wolves *(Don't go with the crowd)*   100
16 Snow White and the Dwarfs *(Be considerate)*   104
17 Alfred and the Cakes *(Keep your cool)*   108
18 Mean Jean *(Help when you can)*   111
19 Plain Jane *(Fight worry with faith)*   115
20 Lazy Maisie *(Don't make excuses)*   120
21 The Traveller *(Be fair)*   123
22 The Journey *(Be generous)*   127
23 The Blabbermouth *(Don't gossip)*   130
24 Goodbye, Mr Bigshot *(Learn to listen)*   134
25 The Bishop and the Britons *(Take advice)*   137
26 Toy Story *(Don't give up)*   140
27 A Human for Christmas *(Be kind to animals)*   144
28 The Three Builders *(Build wisely)*   148

Part Three: COMMITMENT-BUILDING STORIES

Key stories from the life of Jesus

29 From Heaven to Earth *(The angel's story)*   155
30 The Best Moment of her Life *(Anna's story)*   160
31 Voice in the Desert *(John's story)*   163
32 The Wedding Feast *(Mary's story)*   167
33 Big Catch – New Job *(Simon's story)*   171
34 In a Stew *(Martha's story)*   175
35 Is She, or Isn't She? *(Jairus' story)*   179
36 Straightened Out *(Zacchaeus' story)*   183
37 Nadab is Shocked *(The Pharisee's story)*   187
38 Hidden Treasure *(The widow's story)*   191
39 What Kind of a King Washes Feet? *(Judas' story)*   195
40 Execution Day *(The centurion's story)*   199
41 Why – What – How – Where?
    (Mary Magdalene's story)   203
42 Comings, Goings and Coming Again
    (The mountain's story)   207

Part Four: KINGDOM-BUILDING STORIES

True stories of faith in action

43 The Wee Ginger Boy *(Forgiving)*   213
44 A Truly Happy Christmas *(Praying and witnessing)*   217
45 No Good at Sums *(Healing)*   221
46 Rebecca's Wheelchair *(Caring)*   225
47 One for Nan *(Encouraging)*   230
48 Lali and Moni *(Using gifts and abilities)*   234
49 The Street Sale *(Fundraising)*   238
50 Lighter and Brighter *(Sharing in work and worship)*   242

Subject Index   247
Scripture Index   251

Acknowledgements

Many thanks to the friends and acquaintances who generously provided information for the stories in the Kingdom-building section of this book; they include Brian Callan, Sam and David Campbell, John and Jackie Chaplin, Hilary Clegg, Jan and Rachel Dyer, Tim Hamilton, Jill Harshaw and Jonathan Rea.

I'd also like to thank the children and leaders of Finaghy Methodist Sunday School, in particular Deidre McHugh, for inspiring the opening sequence of stories.

Thanks, too, to Philip Saunders for his help and encouragement, and to the Idle household for allowing me to visit their gecko!

Last but not least come the cohabitants of the family building site. Thank you, Christopher and Patrick, for your continued enthusiasm for stories, and thank you, David, for your continued love and support.

Introduction

My father is an architect. My grandfather was a builder. I'm in the construction business too, although not with bricks and mortar. My building site is the family home where the buildings going up are the lives of my children.

Every builder knows the importance of solid foundations. For foundations to be solid where life-building is concerned, the bricks must be cemented with the knowledge of right and wrong. A recent survey showed that the majority of parents thought that honesty was a key value they wished to instil in their children. I, too, want my offspring to know they shouldn't lie or steal, and that they should own up to wrongdoing. This means I'm engaged in conscience-building. But more important I want them to discover the rich rewards of doing what is right. My desire is that they should be generous, considerate, fair, helpful and reliable, not because they *have* to but because they prefer to. So hand in hand with the work of conscience-building goes the work of character-building.

In theory this sounds attainable – as if all that parents and teachers need to do is invest time and energy in the building process, and their children's lives will go up according to plan. In practice, the mud and mess of the human condition means

11

slipping and sliding along the way. It may even precipitate total collapse. So I want children to know why we need spiritual help and where to get it. I want them to be clear about God's plan for pulling us out of the mud. I want them to understand who Jesus is, why he came, what he did, and how he can change, empower and give meaning and purpose to life.

We're into commitment and kingdom-building here. For Jesus isn't just a historical figure. He's someone to be encountered personally today; someone to be followed, known and shared in the nitty-gritty of experience. So I long that both my own children and the children I meet with in church and in schools should make this glorious discovery – something more caught than taught – and continue to be built up in it for the rest of their days.

Surely this is God's desire too – to see healthy moral and spiritual development take place in the lives of the millions of children growing up in the world. And surely one of the tools he gives Christian parents and leaders for the task is the tool of storytelling. Jesus used it and it's there for us too – a tool which allows us to teach without preaching, to touch sensitive spots without awkwardness, to explore actions and choices without risk.

The stories in this book come under four headings: Conscience-building, Character-building, Commitment-building and Kingdom-building. They are designed to help adults help children erect a sturdy moral and spiritual framework for their lives.

A talking/teaching point and a Bible reference accompanies every story. Notes on how to tell particular stories, follow-up activities, background information, song suggestions (from the *Children's Ministry Songbook* to be published January 2002), or short prayers are also sometimes included. It is my prayer that the book may prove useful, and that users may know the blessing of the Master Builder as they teach and guide the children in their care.

Part One

CONSCIENCE-BUILDING STORIES

The Castle –
a story series introducing the Ten Commandments

These stories are designed to be read aloud with children, either at home or in a church/school group. Approximate age range: 6–10.

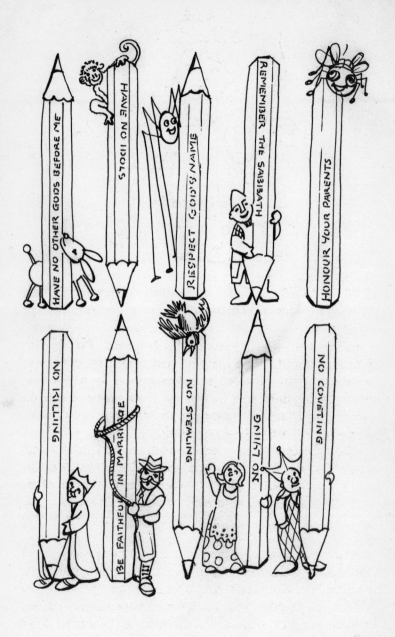

1. Laws for Living

Jonathan Jones had a castle in his bedroom. The fine toy building, topped with battlements and turrets, sat in pride of place on the toy-cupboard. It had been there for almost four years. A drawbridge led up to the main entrance and the whole front came off to show the tower rooms, throne-room, courtyard, kitchen and dungeons inside.

The castle had come complete with model figures – four knights, a dog, a king, a servant-girl and a clown. Jonathan called the king Arthur, and the knights Eenie, Meenie, Minie and Mo. He called the dog Sausage and the clown Coco, but he didn't bother naming the servant because he didn't use her in his games.

Something else Jonathan didn't use much was the set of colouring pencils Great Aunt Jemima had given him for Christmas. 'Colour with the Commandments' it said on the box. When Jonathan took out the pencils he discovered they had Bible verses – the Ten Commandments – printed down

15

the side. None of his classmates had pencils like that, so the box ended up on top of the toy cupboard with the castle.

Time passed. The box gathered dust and so did the castle. Then, one Monday, the castle figures heard Jonathan tell his mum he'd swapped a poster for some football stickers at school. On Tuesday the boy swapped a rubber for a comic. On Wednesday he looked round the bedroom for something to swap. Suddenly he noticed the castle. 'I hardly ever play with that now,' he muttered. Next thing, he'd plucked King Arthur from the throne room and gone off with him in his pocket.

It happened that quickly. One minute everything was normal and the next – disaster! The castle figures could hardly take it in. Their good king gone! Snatched away from them without warning. In the kitchen, the servant-girl buried her head in her apron and wept, while in the throne room the shocked knights stood around, staring at the empty throne.

'Oh, oh, oh!' Mo, the smallest knight wailed. 'We're undone! What will we do without our King?'

Eenie, Meenie and Minie squared their shoulders and tried to look the way knights should in an emergency.

'It's all right, Mo.' Tall, fair Eenie marched towards the throne. 'I'll take charge of things.'

'Not so fast!' Meenie and Minie blocked his way. 'Why should you be the one to sit on the throne?'

'That's obvious.' Eenie pulled himself up to his full height. 'I'm the biggest.'

'So what?' yelled Meenie. 'I'm the brainiest.'

'But I'm the fiercest. The throne is mine!' Warlike Minie drew his sword.

'Help! They're going to fight,' wailed Mo.

Just then a figure dived nose-first into the throne room. It was Coco, the clown, armed with a pencil. 'Stop that at once!' He jammed the pencil into the group of knights and pushed them apart. 'Our king has only been gone five minutes and already you're behaving like humans.'

At these words, the knights hung their heads.

'That's better,' said Coco. 'Now, two things are clear. First, King Arthur isn't here, and second we need someone to lead us wisely and bravely through the difficult days ahead.'

'Me!' cried Eenie.

'No, me!' cried Meenie.

'It's a fight to the death,' Minie yelled.

The clown silenced them with a wave of the pencil. 'Listen! The toymaker who carved us painted a golden crown on King Arthur's head. He was made to be a king. I was given an orange nose and made to be a clown. You got helmets and armour, so you were made to be knights. And the maid was given an apron, so she was made to serve. Agreed?'

The knights nodded.

'Well then, here's my idea. Serving means doing what's needed, and what is needed now is someone to make decisions until we can get our king back. I say we should ask the maid to rule over us.'

There was a short silence. Then. . . 'Why not?' Eenie shrugged.

'She wouldn't annoy anyone,' said Meenie.

'And she's a good cook,' said Mo. 'I'll get her.'

So the maid was brought from the kitchen to the throne room. 'Me? Sit on the throne? Have you all gone crazy?' Her round, black eyes almost popped out of her head. 'I'm just the maid. That isn't even a proper name.'

'We could change it,' said Eenie. 'You could be Helen or Sarah or Kate. . .'

'Or Dearest,' said Mo. 'Jonathan's mum is called Dearest.'

'No she isn't,' sighed Meenie. 'That's just what Jonathan's dad calls her. Her real name is Laura – and before you ask, his dad's name isn't Darling. It's Henry.'

'Henry. . .' repeated Mo. 'Henry. That's a good name. We could call the maid Henry.'

'Well, Henry, what do you think?' Coco smiled.

'You're joking!' The rosy-cheeked doll in her polka dot skirt shook her head.

Just then Coco noticed the small stamp on the bottom of her apron. He already knew what it said. The castle figures all had a stamp like that somewhere on their surfaces. Now, though, it gave him an idea. 'How about this! It says "Handmade in China" on your apron. You're a maid and "made in" sounds like Maiden. So why don't we call you Maiden China?'

'Maiden China!' The doll clapped in delight. 'That's exactly the name I've been waiting for.'

'Great!' beamed Mo. 'She's got a name. We've got a ruler.'

But already the flush of excitement had left Maiden China's cheeks. 'I'll need more than a good name if I'm to sit on the throne,' she said quietly. 'King Arthur made wise decisions because he had a crown on his head and a heart of gold. I have nothing to help me.'

'Yes you have,' said Coco. 'Come this way and I'll show you.'

Taking the doll by the hand, he led her across the drawbridge and over to the far corner of the cupboard where the 'Colour with the Commandments' box sat. With a deft kick, he flipped the lid open and Maiden China found herself looking down on a rainbow-coloured row of well-sharpened pencils. She counted nine. Then Coco slipped the white one he'd used to separate the knights into its place. That made ten altogether. Ten pencils, all with words in gold letters written down the sides. 'There are laws for living written on these pencils,' said Coco. 'Laws given to humans by their Maker. When you need help, these pencils will guide you.'

A few moments later they returned to the throne room.

'Well, Maiden China, what is your answer?' asked Eenie.

'You can make brilliant crumb-cakes. Please say you'll make decisions too!' begged Mo.

Sighing, the doll turned towards the empty throne. Really, all she wanted was to return to the kitchen. But she could feel six pairs of eyes upon her, urging her forward.

'Oh all right. I'll do it.' She hauled herself up into the broad golden chair. 'Just as long as you remember I'm not used to ruling. We must all pull together and get by the best we can.'

'All pull together and buy the best can,' echoed Mo. 'Hey! That's a brilliant idea! If we buy the best watering can, we can make a nice damp vegetable patch on Jonathan's wallpaper and grow our own mould.'

Mo's words brought a faint smile to Maiden China's lips. 'What I meant is that we must all help each other until our king gets back.'

'Oh, right. . . I see.' The small knight looked disappointed. 'Well, that's a good idea too, I suppose.'

So the question of who was to sit on the throne was peacefully settled. Still, up until the moment Jonathan came home from school Maiden China felt as if it was a game of make-believe. 'Any minute now, Jonathan will take King Arthur out of his pocket,' she thought. 'Any minute now, things will get back to normal.' But they didn't. Jonathan took something out of his pocket all right. But it wasn't the king. It was a glistening sugar doughnut. A doughnut! The figures gaped. He'd swapped their king for a doughnut!

As Jonathan crammed the doughnut into his mouth, he spotted the 'Colour with the Commandments' box lying open on the cupboard. 'Hmm,' the boy muttered stickily. 'I'm sure I didn't leave it that way. Mum's been in here fiddling with my pencils.'

Talking point

Before the story, show the children the illustrations of the eight characters. (All illustrations may be photocopied for use with a group). Afterwards, refer to the illustration of the pencils with the texts. Talk about the Ten Commandments, explaining how God gave them to Moses. Say that they were first written down on tablets of stone. With older children, look up Exodus 20:1–17 in the Bible so that they know where the Ten Commandments are found.

Bible base

Exodus 20:1–17

Prayer

Dear Father, thank you that in the Bible we find laws to guide us. Help us pay attention to the things you say. Amen.

2. The Blue Pencil
(No other gods before me)

The next day Sausage the dog had an accident. He was out chasing sunbeams along the top of the cupboard when a bluebottle zoomed across his path. Sausage dodged to avoid it and crashed into the wall. Suddenly a crack appeared round his tummy. With a tiny snap his hind legs fell off and disappeared down the back of the cupboard. It was every toy's worst nightmare. 'Oh no! I'm broken,' Sausage yelped. He couldn't walk. He couldn't scratch. He didn't even have a tail. What really worried him, though, was the Cowboys and Indians' latest rule – a rule which said broken toys must be thrown out.

Shivering with fear, the dog crawled back to the castle, and tried to shuffle across the drawbridge without being seen. But it was no good. He couldn't hide the fact that half of him had gone missing. Eenie, Meenie, Minie and Mo were down from the battlements in an instant.

'Where are your back legs?' asked Eenie.

'It doesn't take a genius like me to see that you've lost

them,' said Meenie.

'You know the new rule,' Minie grabbed what was left of Sausage by the scruff of the neck. 'The Cowboys and Indians won't let us shelter a broken toy. We'll have to throw you out.'

This was just what Sausage had been afraid of. 'No! No! I won't let the Cowboys and Indians see me. Please let me stay,' he howled.

The noise brought Maiden China and Coco running from the throne room.

'Your Maidship, we must get rid of Sausage the dog. He's broken and that's the rule,' cried Eenie.

'Don't listen to them, Maiden China!' said Coco. 'King Arthur never agreed to any such rule. He wasn't afraid of the Cowboys and Indians. Sausage belongs here.'

'Not any more he doesn't,' said Eenie. 'If we keep him, we'll be attacked.'

'And outnumbered!' Minie drew his sword. 'Just think! Over fifty Cowboys and Indians against six and a half of us.'

'What are we to do, Your Maidship?' asked Coco.

It was Maiden China's first big test. 'Let me see. . .' Her mind was racing. She had to give an order. But first she had to work out what to say. She certainly didn't want to get rid of Sausage, but she didn't want a war either. So should she get rid of the dog to save the castle? Or risk the castle to save the dog?

Suddenly the doll remembered the box of coloured pencils.

'Before I decide, we must read the laws,' she said. 'Mo, please go and fetch a pencil.'

A few minutes later, Mo was back. He had a very confused look on his face and a blue pencil under his arm. 'Your Maidship, I've brought you the first pencil, but I don't think you'll be able to understand it. The law doesn't make sense. It says "Me before gods other no have".'

'Me before gods other no have,' Meenie repeated slowly. 'Me before gods other no have. . . ah yes, yes indeed. Those words may not make sense to a pea-brain like you, dear Mo, but to my mind, they are full of meaning.'

'Are they?' Mo laid the pencil on the ground and everyone gathered round.

'Allow me to explain.' Meenie's chest swelled with importance. 'This law falls neatly into two parts. The first part, "Me before gods", describes the way many humans act in the world today. They put themselves first – before anyone and anything else. Me first. That's their motto. They think they're the greatest.' He took a deep breath and continued grandly. 'Then, in the second part of the verse, we see the result of such behaviour: "other no have". When humans put themselves first, some get everything they want, and others "no have". In other words, they get nothing. Quite simply, dear Mo, this law describes what happens when humans are selfish.'

While Meenie was speechifying, Maiden China had been trying to get a word in edgeways. At last she succeeded. 'I'm sorry Meenie, but you and Mo are reading the commandments back to front. This law doesn't say "Me before gods other no have". It says "Have no other gods before me".'

'That's right,' grinned Coco. 'This is the Mighty Maker talking – telling humans he's the greatest and they mustn't put anyone or anything before him.'

'Oh, of course. Silly me! Silly Meenie! Now I understand,' Mo beamed.

Meenie gave a splutter. 'As I was saying, this law is full of meaning whatever way we read it. It tells humans not to act selfishly and to put their Maker first.'

There was a moment of silence, then Sausage whimpered. 'But does it say who decides what happens to a broken dog?'

Even as the dog spoke, a thought popped into Maiden China's head. If humans were meant to put the Mighty Maker first, then surely toys should put their owners first.

'This pencil makes me think we should let Jonathan decide what to do about Sausage,' she said slowly.

'But he hardly ever plays with us now,' frowned Eenie. 'It

could be months before he notices Sausage is broken.'

'Then we must make him notice,' cried Mo. 'How about us all jumping up and down on the battlements when he's doing his homework. He'd notice us then, for sure.'

'He'd think he'd gone mad,' said Meenie. 'And if he talked about it, everyone else would think he was mad too.'

Maiden China looked around the room, searching for a way out of the difficulty. 'I know,' she said suddenly. 'I know how to make Jonathan notice what's happened without driving him mad. Go into the castle, Meenie, and fetch the roll of spider thread we keep in the corner of the courtyard.'

Meenie brought the thread and Maiden China took it over to the edge of the cupboard. She tied the loose end round a splinter of wood and dropped the rest of the coil down to the floor. 'Here's the plan,' she said. 'We're going to slide down the thread onto the carpet. Coco, you're good at acrobatics, so you can carry Sausage under your arm. Knights, once you reach the ground you must collect Sausage's back legs from behind the cupboard and leave them by his side. Then we'll all lie down on the carpet and wait for Jonathan to come home.'

'You mean we're going to lie there as if we have fallen?' the knights gasped. 'But what if the Cowboys and Indians come out and attack us?'

'They won't.' Maiden China sounded braver than she felt. 'They hardly ever wake up before teatime – and Jonathan will have picked us up and made his decision by then.'

'And what if he decides to throw me out?' whined Sausage.

What indeed? Maiden China picked up the broken dog and hugged what was left of him close. 'Let's not even think about that,' she whispered. She did think about it, though. In fact, she thought about little else as they lay there waiting for Jonathan.

At last the bedroom door opened and their owner came into the room. He took one look at the rug, then ran the fingers of one hand through his untidy blond hair so it stuck up like an exclamation mark. What on earth had happened? His castle figures were scattered over the floor and the brown dog was broken.

It was all his mother's fault, the boy decided. Yesterday, she'd fiddled with his pencils and today she must have opened a window to clear the air of smelly feet. Only she hadn't just got rid of the cheesy smell, had she? No, she'd done real damage this time.

With an exasperated shrug, the boy went over to his desk. He wrote the words 'KEEP OUT' on a piece of paper, and stuck the notice on his bedroom door. Then he began to clear up the mess. He picked up the figures and put the knights, the clown and the servant girl straight back into the castle. 'Now what do I do with this?' He stood cradling Sausage's front end in one hand and his back end in the other.

Maiden China held her breath. 'Jonathan isn't selfish,' she told herself. 'He's the sort of boy who puts his Maker first. I'm sure I was right to trust him.'

And, to her great relief, Jonathan didn't toss Sausage into the waste-paper basket. Instead, he went back to his desk and took a tube of superglue out of the drawer. Pushing his glasses up on his nose, he squeezed a small, clear globule of glue onto Sausage's legs. He pressed the legs against the rest of the dog's body. 'There. That should do the trick,' he said.

It did.

The glue hardened. And Sausage was as good as new.

That night there was a party in the castle. Sausage celebrated getting his legs back. And everyone celebrated the success of Maiden China's plan.

At the height of the fun, Mo sidled up to the throne. He pointed to the blue 'Have no other gods before me' pencil, which was lying at Maiden China's feet.

'Your Maidship, the law on that pencil reminds humans not to be selfish and to put their Mighty Maker first. Right?'

'Right.' Maiden China wondered what was coming.

'Well, Your Maidship, I've got two questions – a big

question and little question,' said Mo. 'Number one: I've been wondering what humans need to do to keep that law?'

'Goodness, Mo!' Maiden China struggled to find an answer. 'I suppose they keep it by learning about the Mighty Maker. And by trusting him and trying to do what he wants. But, like you said, it's a very big question.'

'Oh, that's my little question,' beamed Mo. 'My big question is. . . I was wondering. . . well, I was wondering. . .' The small knight took a deep breath. 'I was wondering who would be the one to carry the pencil back across the cupboard.'

'It should be me. I'm the biggest,' cried Eenie.

'No, me! I'm the brainiest,' cried Meenie.

'I'm the fiercest.' Minie waved his sword.

Maiden China picked up the blue pencil. 'I have decided this pencil should be carried back across the cupboard by the knight who fetched it in the first place.'

'Hey! That's me!' squeaked Mo.

'So it is.' Maiden China handed him the pencil. Then, together, they walked across the cupboard to put it back in the 'Colour with the Commandments' box.

Talking point

See if the children remember the colour of the pencil in the story (blue). They can then turn to the pencil illustration and colour the first pencil in. Explain how, many years ago, God's people had been slaves in the land of Egypt, surrounded by Egyptians who worshipped other gods. The Israelites had continued to believe in the One True God – and he had helped them escape. Talk about what it means to believe in God and put him first today.

Bible base

Exodus 20:1–3

Prayer

Dear Father, thank you that you are bigger and greater than we can ever imagine. Help us to put you and what you want first in our lives. Amen.

3. The Red Pencil
(No idols)

Maiden China woke up next morning feeling worried. For a moment she couldn't remember the reason why. Then it came back to her. Their beloved king had vanished, and she was in charge. Her heart sank. Being in charge made everything so different. Jonathan was still fast asleep in bed, but today she couldn't just smile at the way he'd dropped off with a comic over his face; she had to use these few minutes to think of things for the knights to do. Should she get them to spring-clean the castle? No, that was too risky. Jonathan – or, more likely, Jonathan's mum – might notice that the dust had disappeared. Maiden China sighed. How she longed for their real ruler to return.

The king was still in her thoughts as she joined the figures for breakfast. 'I think we should send King Arthur a letter to cheer him up,' she announced. 'We'll address it to Kate's house. Kate's mum is a baker, so it should reach him there.'

'I don't follow,' frowned Mo.

28

'Yes you do,' said Coco. 'Kate is in Jonathan's class at school. Her mum owns a bakery. Just think what a baker's daughter would be likely to swap.'

'Doughnuts!' beamed Mo. 'I know. Let's address the letter to Kate's house. She's the person in Jonathan's class most likely to have the king.'

'Well done, Mo!' Coco winked.

So Maiden China and Coco went over to the box of pencils. They took out the red pencil and tried to decide what to write. 'What do you say to someone who has been swapped for a doughnut?' Maiden China wondered.

Coco scratched his head. 'I'm not sure. How about: "Dear King, we miss you. We hope you'll be swapped back soon."'

'That sounds good. We do miss him very much,' Maiden China agreed.

Meanwhile, back at the castle, a brown furry visitor had arrived. It was Micky, the stuffed monkey, and he was full of doom and gloom.

'You got problem,' he warned. 'Cowboys and Indians come dig for gold in these parts. They turn top of toy cupboard into Wild West.'

At the thought of what this would mean, the knights went pale. 'They'll build ranches,' said Meenie.

'And drive heavy wagons,' said Eenie.

'And rustle cattle,' said Minie.

'You mean they'll make cows act like leaves,' gasped Mo. 'That's wicked! Making cattle rustle when they're meant to moo!'

'Too right,' said Micky. 'But me know how to stop them.'

'How?' cried Mo.

'Me show you. Come outside,' said Micky.

Leaving Sausage on guard, Eenie, Meenie, Minie and Mo followed the monkey outside the castle. There, propped against the wall, they saw what looked like a cream-coloured log.

'What's that?' Meenie pointed.

'No! No! You no point.' Micky caught his arm. 'You give bowing-down honour to elephant's tooth.'

'You mean that. . . that cream thing is an elephant's tooth?' squeaked Mo.

Micky nodded. 'Too right. Jungle cousin send me tooth from mouth of mighty white elephant. You honour it most respectfully – like so.' He lay flat on the ground. 'You too. You bow down.'

The knights lay flat. 'Now you say words,' the monkey ordered. 'Oh tooth, oh great jungle tooth, protect this cupboard, we pray.'

'Oh tooth, oh great jungle tooth, protect this cupboard, we pray,' the knights repeated. 'Say again,' said Micky. And they said it again. 'Now you getty up,' said Micky.

The knights got up and dusted themselves down. 'Cupboard all safe now,' grinned Micky. 'Cowboys and Indians no match for jungle power.'

'Phew!' Mo mopped his brow. 'That's a relief!'

'So we do business?' Micky rubbed his paws. 'Me can't *give* away elephant's tooth, you know. Great, cupboard-protecting tooth cost you six marbles.'

The knights looked at each other. 'OK,' Eeenie nodded. 'It's a deal.'

Just as the knights were about to hand over the marbles, Coco and Maiden China arrived home. The letter to the king was finished, and Maiden China had brought the red pencil so everyone could sign it. She was surprised to see Micky, and even more surprised to see the elephant's tooth.

Solemnly, and using a lot of impressive words like 'major threat' and 'necessary precautions', Meenie passed on Micky's warning about the Cowboys and Indians. 'It's all right, though,' he finished reassuringly. 'All we need to do is bow down to this tooth and it will keep us safe.'

'Tooth keepy you safe,' nodded Micky. 'All safe for six marbles.'

Maiden China looked into the monkey's grinning face.

King Arthur had never trusted Micky, she knew. But it was the three words written on the pencil at her feet that helped her make up her mind – 'Have no idols', they said. 'Sorry, Monkey. I'm in charge around here. And the commandment tells me to have nothing to do with this.' She marched over to the tooth and kicked it flat on the ground.

The knights gasped in horror.

'But the pencil doesn't say anything about teeth,' protested Eenie, pointing to the gold lettering on the side. 'It says: "Have no idols".'

'And the tooth isn't an idol – it's a tooth,' cried Mo.

'Listen, Mo, this commandment means that humans should only worship the Maker who is too big to be seen,' said Maiden China. 'An idol can be anything that takes his place. Humans shouldn't trust idols to keep them safe and we toys shouldn't trust teeth.'

'Especially when they are made of chalk,' grinned Coco.

'Chalk?' gasped the knights.

'That's right!' Coco lifted the tooth and drew a powdery X on the floor. 'Chalk is what Micky's so-called tooth is made of. It's a fake. And my guess is that his warnings about Cowboys and Indians are fake too.'

'Well, Micky, what have you got to say for yourself?' Maiden China faced the monkey.

Micky immediately dropped to the ground and scrabbled humbly at her feet. 'OK. Me confess. Me make up story. Me thinky me could tricky knights. But knights too clever. Clown too clever. Doll too clever. Me cross with Micky. Micky very bad and silly monkey.' He smacked himself on the paw.

'Get up, Micky,' said Maiden China. 'And don't ever try anything like that again.'

'Too right.' Micky grinned and leapt to his feet. 'Me no try makey marbles ever. . . ever. . . Me good monkey now. Bye, bye.' He picked up the chalk and swung down from the toy cupboard onto the floor.

Eenie, Meenie, Minie and Mo were furious.

'Him and his rotten tooth!' they raged. 'Imagine thinking we'd be stupid enough to fall for a stunt like that!'

A little later, when the knights had stopped fuming, Maiden China got out the letter to the king. By the time Jonathan's alarm clock went off, the letter was signed and ready to be dropped into his schoolbag. Everyone stood along the edge of the cupboard, watching the little piece of white paper flutter down among the books. 'I suppose,' said Mo, 'when Jonathan gets to school his teacher will say: "Now boys and girls, please open your bags and take out the letters your toys want you to send." '

'You're so dim, Mo,' Meenie sighed. 'Of course the teacher won't say that.'

'Um. . . so how will the king get our letter?' asked Mo.

'He won't. We're wasting our time,' muttered Meenie.

'No we aren't,' said Maiden China. 'Bowing down to a tooth was a waste of time, but now we're doing the right thing – and time is never wasted doing that.'

Talking point

The children colour in the red pencil and look at the text. Ask them what the colour red makes them think of (danger). Talk about the different things we do that help us feel safe – locking doors, sleeping with a light on etc. Point out that people sometimes do superstitious things – like wearing a lucky charm, or trusting a horoscope – which is a bit like bowing down to idols. The second commandment reminds us that we can trust God to look after us and keep us safe.

Bible base

Exodus 20:4–5

Prayer

Dear Father, thank you that even though we cannot see you, we know that you are there. Whenever we feel worried or afraid, help us to put our trust in you. Amen.

4. The Black Pencil
(Respect God's name)

First thing on Saturday morning a sparrow hopped onto the window-ledge with some good news. 'The king got your message,' it chirped. 'The letter is still in Jonathan's bag, but it was read by a beetle who passed the message on to a bee. The bee passed it on to a spider living in Kate's house and the spider promised to take it to the king.'

Maiden China was thrilled. Knowing they'd got a message through to King Arthur brought him closer, somehow. 'We owe a great deal to those insects,' she said. 'I wish we could show them how grateful we are.'

'We could write a card to the bee. Bees are nice. They make honey,' said Mo.

'Or how about inviting all the insects to a singsong?' said Coco. 'Insects always enjoy humming along.'

'Especially bees,' said Mo.

'I've a better idea,' said Eenie. 'Let's give them a guided tour of the castle.'

'Let's do all three,' said Maiden China. 'Let's write a card inviting the insects to a guided tour, and end it with a singsong.'

So Mo fetched the black pencil from the 'Colour with the Commandments' box, and printed out a notice.

TOUR OF BUILDING
AFTER BREAKFAST
JUST BUZZ

'I put three words beginning with B in the notice because I wanted bees to know they were specially welcome,' he explained.

'All insects are especially welcome, Mo,' said Maiden China. 'But the notice sounds fine. Go and lay it flat on the ground outside the castle so our insect friends can view it from the air.'

The notice went out, but time passed and there wasn't a visitor to be seen.

'That's the trouble with insects,' growled Minie, 'all they ever want to do is swarm round picnics.'

Coco shrugged. 'Mo should have mentioned the singsong. That would have brought them in.'

Just then there was a buzz at the door.

It turned out to be a daddy-long-legs and two flies. 'We're here to tour the breakfast,' they buzzed.

'You mean you're here to tour the castle,' smiled Eenie.

'Well, that too. But it does say on your notice: Tour of Breakfast – After Building, so we thought breakfast was the main thing.'

'Ooops!' Mo looked guilty. 'Maybe I shouldn't have changed the words round.'

'Of course you shouldn't! It's not just the sound words make that matters; you've got to think about the meaning,' Coco hissed.

The insects were split into groups for the guided tour.

Maiden China decided that she and Coco would take care of the daddy-long-legs while the two flies went with the knights. 'The daddy-long-legs is group A and the flies are group B,' she began.

'No, no, Your Maidship, the flies can't be bees,' interrupted Mo.

'I didn't say they were bees, Mo. I said they were group B.'

'But even if they are in a group – they're still flies, not bees.'

'Very well,' sighed Maiden China. 'The flies are group C. Group A will start in the dungeons and work up to the top of the tower. And group C will start at the top of the tower and work down to the dungeons.'

This plan went smoothly. The daddy-long-legs was a perfect guest – polite, well-behaved, never once getting his legs in a tangle. The flies, though, were very loud. Every time the knights took them to a different part of the castle, they would race each other to see who would get there first, and the one who lost would call the winner a meanie. 'Meanie, meanie, meanie,' they would buzz.

The first time this happened Meenie the knight looked cross.

The second time it happened he looked very cross.

And the third time it happened he stormed off with a face like thunder.

When the insects left, Maiden China called everyone into the throne room to say well done. But before she could open her mouth Meenie blurted out: 'I want to alter my appellation.'

'I'll get you a needle and thread,' offered Mo. 'It's horrible when your appellation gets too tight.'

'An appellation is a name, Mo,' hissed Coco. 'He means he wants to change his name.'

The other knights gasped. This was the last thing they'd expected.

'But why?' asked Maiden China.

'Because nobody respects it,' cried Meenie. 'You heard those flies. All sorts of creatures call each other meanies and they never think about me. So I've decided I don't want to be called Meenie. From now on you can call me Einstein.'

At this Mo's chin began to wobble. 'Don't allow it, Maiden China. Him being Einstein would be horrid. We wouldn't be Eenie, Meenie, Minie and Mo any more.'

Maiden China frowned. 'Mo has a point. "Eenie, Meenie, Minie, Mo" just slips off the tongue but "Eenie, Einstein, Minie, Mo" doesn't.'

'Do you want me to fetch a pencil, Your Maidship?' Coco asked, seeing that she faced a difficult decision.

'Please,' Maiden China nodded. 'The black one Mo used to write the notice is still over there in the corner.'

Coco fetched the pencil.

'It says here, "Respect God's name".' Eenie read the words on the side.

'That means the Mighty Maker's name is special and humans shouldn't say it without thinking, ' said Coco.

'Right. They should only use it when they're speaking to him or talking about him,' Maiden China nodded.

'But what does the pencil mean for *me*?' asked Meenie.

'I think it reminds us that names are important,' said Maiden China. 'Meenie was the special name that Jonathan gave you. I'm sure he wouldn't want you to change it over the foolish buzzing of two silly flies.'

Everyone held their breath while Meenie thought this over.

'Oh all right,' he nodded. 'I'll keep my own name.'

'Hurrah! That's settled then!' cheered Mo.

Maiden China picked up the pencil.

'I'll tell you something good,' she told Coco, as they slipped it back into the 'Colour with the Commandments' box. 'I've never once heard Jonathan misuse the Mighty Maker's name.'

'Yes, it *is* good he tries to keep the commandments,' Coco agreed. 'Even if he doesn't colour with them much.'

Talking point

The children colour in the black pencil and look at the text: 'Respect God's name.' Make sure they understand that mis-using God's name means saying 'God' or 'Jesus' when we aren't speaking about him or praying to him. Talk about their own names and what they like or do not like to be called. The way someone uses our name can show their attitude towards us. The way we use God's name will show our attitude to him.

Bible base

Exodus 20:7

Prayer

Dear Father, thank you that each of us is special and that we each have our own name that is known to you. Please help us not to use names hurtfully. Help us especially not to misuse your name. Amen.

5. The Yellow Pencil
(Remember the Sabbath)

On Sunday morning Minie and Mo couldn't wait to show another group of insects around the castle. Eenie and Meenie, however, weren't keen. They didn't mind opening up the castle once or twice a week, but not day after day after day.

'Spoil-sports! We want the castle open,' cried Minie.

'Slave-drivers! We want it closed,' argued Eenie.

'Open.'

'Closed.'

'Open.'

'Closed.'

Maiden China could see they'd have no peace until she made a decision, so she asked Coco to fetch a pencil.

A few moments later Coco came back empty-handed and announced that the pencils weren't in their usual place.

'Not in their usual place!' cried Maiden China. 'You mean they've disappeared?'

Coco nodded and Maiden China wrung her apron. 'This is

terrible. I can't decide things without the pencils.'

'My superior brain tells me that pencils don't simply disappear into thin air,' said Meenie. 'I say we should go outside and look for them.'

Everyone raced outside and started to hunt.

'There they are!' Eeenie shouted suddenly. 'Look, the box is poking up out of the pocket of Jonathan's jacket.'

Jonathan's jacket was hanging over the back of the chair by the desk, and, yes, the 'Colour with the Commandments' box was in the pocket. Maiden China put two and two together. 'It's Sunday. Jonathan must be taking the pencils to church.'

'Don't worry, Your Maidship,' cried Mo. 'I'll hide in the pocket and learn the pencils off by heart. That way, even if Jonathan swaps them in church we'll remember what they said.'

With these words, he raced off across the cupboard and took a flying leap into Jonathan's jacket pocket. Even as he leapt, the figures heard the sound of footsteps on the stairs. 'Quick! Into the castle, everyone,' cried Coco. 'Jonathan's coming.'

There was nothing else for it. Maiden China, the three knights, Coco and Sausage had to scramble up to the battlements. They looked on helplessly as Jonathan raced into the room, rubbed a smear of chocolate spread off his face, pulled on his jacket and left.

There was a moment of silence.

Then Sausage howled, Eeenie groaned and Meenie heaved a deep sigh.

'Gone. . . gone. . . gone. . .' groaned Eenie. 'First our beloved king and now our dear, foolish Mo.'

'King Arthur always told us to look after Mo,' sighed Meenie. 'And now Maiden China's let him be carried away.'

'It's up to us to search for him,' growled Minie. 'Come on, brothers.' He marshalled Eenie and Meenie into line and next thing they were marching from the battlements. Left. . . right . . . left. . . right. . .

'This is madness, Your Maidship,' hissed Coco. 'You've got to stop them.'

'Yes. . . yes. . . I know that.' Maiden China picked up her skirts and raced after the knights, with Sausage barking at her heels. She caught up with them at the drawbridge. 'Get back to the battlements,' she ordered. 'I'm sure Jonathan will bring Mo safely home from church. We just have to be patient.'

'No way,' scowled Minie. 'Come on, brothers. . .'

'Get back to the battlements,' Maiden China repeated firmly, 'We're going to have. . . um. . . a talent show.'

A talent show! This was a new idea. In fact, Maiden China wasn't even sure herself where it had come from. It had just popped into her head as she struggled to think how she could stop the knights making a bad situation one hundred times worse.

But it did the trick. The knights trooped back to the battlements and the talent show got under way. First, Sausage showed how well he could walk on his mended hind legs. Then Coco sang a few songs. Then Eenie told a few jokes. (They weren't very funny, but everyone laughed politely.) Minie followed with a dazzling display of swordplay and then it was Meenie's turn.

'Ahem.' He cleared his throat importantly. 'I wish to give a short talk. Ahem. On the classification of insects. Ahem. Yesterday, we gave a successful tour to insects. Ahem. But how much do we really know about them? For example, would it surprise you to learn that the daddy-long-legs who came here was a type of crane fly – not to be confused with the type of crane bird, who wades through water. . . nor yet with the type of crane machine, used for lifting lumps of concrete. . .'

The knight droned on, and his brothers became more and more restless. Suddenly, Minie burst out, 'This is a waste of time. We ought to be out there looking for Mo.'

'Jonathan will be back at any moment,' said Maiden China quickly. 'And anyway, we all want to hear Coco's poem.'

'What poem?' Coco sounded surprised.

'The poem you're going to say for us *now*.' Maiden China looked at him pleadingly.

'Oh *that* poem.' The clown scoured his memory, and managed to recall some verses he'd read in one of Jonathan's Bible story-books. He stood up and began to recite them.

In the beginning there was nothing much to see.
The earth was formless, dark and empty.
Then God, the Creator said: 'Let there be light!'
The world lit up. It was oh so bright!
And God called the light day and the darkness night.

God spent Day Two working on a cover
that would separate one lot of water from another
'Sky,' he called it. It was oh so blue!
Lovely to look at – and useful, too.

On Day Three things really started to happen –
God made the land and sea and loads of vegetation.
On Day Four he got to work on outer space,
close to the earth he put the sun and moon in place.
He made millions upon millions of heavenly powers,
till the sky was like a stadium bursting with stars.

On Day Five came fish and birds to swim and fly about –
eagles and dolphins, budgerigars and trout.
God made oh so many different kinds to fill the air and sea,
and still he was planning more variety
for Day Six saw animals: monkeys and bats,
lions and tigers, guinea pigs and rats,
camels and chameleons, crocodiles and cats
till the earth teemed with life. It was oh such fun!
And still God knew the best had yet to come –
the most brilliant stroke of all in his glorious master plan.
On Day Six it happened – God made man

(and woman, of course) just like himself, but human.
They were oh so special and God just loved them.

Everything was perfect, everything was blessed.
Day Seven dawned. And God had a rest.

Somehow, the poem did the trick. While Coco was speaking, Minie calmed down and listened to every word. 'Thank you, Coco,' Maiden China clapped. 'It's nice to know humans didn't happen by chance, any more than we did.' And with that, the waiting was over.

'Listen! Jonathan's home!' Eenie cried.

Next thing, Jonathan burst into the bedroom. He dumped his jacket on top of the cupboard and dashed off to lay the table for lunch.

No sooner had he shut the door behind him than Mo hopped out of the jacket pocket. 'Hi, guys! Did you give any guided tours while I was gone?' he beamed.

Maiden China wanted both to hug him and shake him at the same time. 'Guided tours! Mo, we've spent the whole morning worrying about you.'

Mo looked more pleased with himself than ever. 'Well, I've spent all morning learning the pencils off by heart,' he said proudly. 'The first commandment is blue, the second is red, the third is black, the fourth is green. . . or maybe it's orange. . . oh dear, I'd better check. . .' Before anyone could speak, he'd disappeared back into the pocket and come out with a pencil. 'Sorry! I got a bit mixed up there. The fourth commandment is yellow,' he said.

The knights burst out laughing, 'Mo, the colours don't matter. It's the words that tell Maiden China what to do.'

'Oops, silly me,' Mo looked at the yellow pencil. 'I forgot to learn the words. But we've still got the pencils, so everything's all right. This one is about washing.' He leapt up onto the battlements and handed the pencil to Coco. 'I'm right, aren't I? The fourth commandment tells humans to remember bath day.'

'Remember the Sabbath day,' Meenie read the words aloud.

'Actually Mo,' said Coco. 'The Sabbath day is about resting, not washing. This pencil reminds us that the Mighty Maker made everything in six days, and then on the Sabbath day he rested. He wants humans to take a day of rest too.'

'That's probably why our humans go to church and Jonathan doesn't do homework on Sunday,' Eenie said.

'I suppose so,' Maiden China nodded. 'What's more, I think it means we should open the castle six days a week, but on Sunday we'll do the same as Jonathan and have a rest.'

Talking point

After the children have coloured in the yellow pencil and looked at the text 'Remember the Sabbath day', find out how many of the commandments they can remember. Point out that in the olden days, when the children of Israel kept the Sabbath, it was one of the ways the nations round about them could see that they belonged to God. Talk about things people do today – such as going to church – that show others God is important to them.

Bible base

Exodus 20:8–11

Prayer

Dear Father, thank you for the wonderful world you made. Help us to see your hand in creation. Thank you for school-days and for holidays. Help us always to make time for you. Amen.

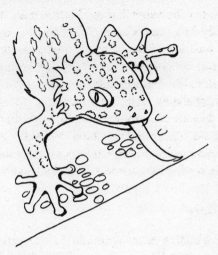

6. The Green Pencil
(Honour your parents)

On Monday morning Jonathan's mum said 'no'. She and Jonathan were talking in the bathroom so the toys couldn't quite hear what she was saying no to – but she said it three times and the third time she said it very loudly indeed. 'Watch my lips, Jonathan. The answer is NO.'

A few moments later, Jonathan stomped into the bedroom like a black cloud in school uniform. 'It's not fair. I'll get that pet anyway,' they heard him mutter as he picked up his bag and went out.

'It appears Jonathan wants a pet of some sort and his mum won't let him have it,' observed Meenie.

'But he's getting it anyway,' said Minie.

'I wonder what it could be?' said Mo.

'I expect we'll find out when he comes home.' Maiden China was looking over the battlements. 'Right now, we've got visitors. A party of ants are on their way up the side of the cupboard.'

The knights lowered the drawbridge only to find that the ants had been joined by four beetles and a very jittery bluebottle.

'Iz it zafe to vizit here?' the bluebottle buzzed nervously. 'Yezterday I toured a pedal bin and almozt got zwatted.'

Minie stepped forward, sword in hand. 'One personal bodyguard at your service, Mr Bluebottle. No insect has ever come to a sticky end under this roof.'

'Oh zank you, zank you.' The bluebottle buzzed in after the other insects, and another successful tour got under way. This time they finished with a singsong in the courtyard. Coco had made up a special song for the occasion.

> Waiter, waiter, there's a fly in my stew,
> a beetle in my soup and a daddy-long-legs too
> And look I see a hairy spider in my pie.
> It makes me want to cry. . .

The bluebottle really enjoyed this and sang enthusiastically at the top of his buzz.

'Zis tour haz really helped me unwind,' he buzzed as he left. 'Your caztle iz a zanctuary for inzects.'

'A sanctuary for insects – did you hear that?' said Minie, proudly waving his sword. 'A sanctuary is a safe place, Mo – in case you were wondering.'

'I wasn't,' said Mo. 'I was thinking about Jonathan. He'll be home soon. I can't wait to see his pet.'

A few minutes later, Jonathan came into the bedroom. He was carrying a box with 'School Hymn-books' written on the side.

'Look, guys! He's got himself a pet hymn-book,' whispered Mo.

'Don't be daft,' Minie hissed.

Next minute, Jonathan's mum popped her head round the door. She noticed the box. 'Are you helping put new covers on the school hymn-books, darling? Good for you!'

Jonathan didn't answer, and when his mum's head disappeared, the figures saw why. He reached into the box and took out a glass-sided tank.

'That's a funny looking hymn-book!' whispered Mo.

'It isn't a hymn-book,' muttered Meenie. 'It's a vivarium – for keeping lizards in. He's got a reptile.'

Sure enough, the boy opened the glass tank and lifted out a skinny, speckled creature with beady black eyes set in a wedge-shaped face. 'Now, Beauty,' the boy whispered, running his forefinger along its back. 'Whatever you do, don't let my mum find you. She hates reptiles. So if a female crumbly called Laura comes into the bedroom, lie low. I'm off to get you a live cricket for tea.' He put the creature back and hid the vivarium behind the castle.

Warily the figures crossed the battlements to examine their new neighbour.

'What kind of lizard is it?' Maiden China asked.

'A gecko, I think,' said Coco.

'They eat crickets,' Meenie groaned. 'You know what that means. The top of the cupboard won't be safe for insects anymore. This creature will kill our business.'

'Don't care,' the gecko said darkly, and stuck out its tongue.

Mo mopped his brow. 'Oh dear! What are we going to do? Maiden China, we'll have to get rid of it.'

'Don't care! Don't care!' the gecko repeated, with a fierce stare.

'Mo's right, Your Maidship,' said Eenie. 'We can't possibly have this creature living beside us on the cupboard. We must open the tank and set it free.'

'But. . . but. . . what if it goes downstairs into the kitchen?' cried Maiden China. 'If Mrs Jones sees it, Jonathan will be in big trouble.'

'Don't care! Don't care!' hissed the gecko.

'It's Jonathan or us, Your Maidship,' said Eenie.

Five days ago, Maiden China would have wrung her apron

over such a big decision. But now she had learnt to stay calm. 'The pencils will help us do what's best,' she said. 'Please go and fetch one.'

Eenie went over to the 'Colour with the Commandments' box. He came back and laid a green pencil down at Maiden China's feet. For a few moments she studied the words on the side. 'Honour your parents,' she repeated them slowly. Then she smiled. 'I think I see how we can keep the cupboard safe, without getting Jonathan into trouble,' she said. 'Eenie, I want you to take this pencil up to the battlements and push it out over the side. Mo, you are to climb onto Coco's shoulders and direct it onto the roof of the tank.'

'But how will a pencil on the tank get rid of Beauty?' wondered Mo.

'I can't explain now. Jonathan will be back soon,' said Maiden China. 'Hurry, please.'

So Eenie took the green pencil and passed it across the battlements. Mo climbed onto Coco's shoulders and steered it onto the vivarium. 'Hey, I know why we're doing this,' he squeaked. 'This pencil says "Honour your parents" but geckos can't read well, so Beauty will think it says "On our land you pay rent". Once he realises we charge rent on our cupboard he won't want to stay. We're letting him know there's no such thing as a free cricket.'

'I'm right, aren't I, Maiden China?' he checked, once he was back on the battlements. 'We've put the pencil on the tank to tell Beauty to pay rent.'

'No, Mo,' smiled Maiden China. 'It isn't there for Beauty, it's there for Jonathan. . . Shhh now, he's coming.'

Sure enough, the pencil was the first thing Jonathan noticed when he came over to feed his new pet. Surprised, he lifted it up. 'Honour your parents' – the three words on the side caught his eye. He reddened, glanced at the green pencil, then glanced at the speckled gecko, then glanced back at the pencil – as if he was trying to decide what to do. Suddenly, he seemed to make up his mind. 'Sorry, Beauty, you can't stay here,' he sighed. 'I can't keep you without Mum's permission.' He put the vivarium back into the cardboard box and away he went.

'Hurrah!' cheered the knights. 'Well done, Your Maidship!'

'You mean "Well done, Jonathan,"' Maiden China smiled. 'The "Honour your parents" pencil reminded him that children are meant to obey their mums and dads. I'm so glad he decided to do the right thing.'

'He won't regret it,' said Minie. 'That gecko had a mean streak. It would never have made a good pet.'

'Whereas Mrs Jones *is* a good parent,' said Eenie.

'Yes, she may hate reptiles but she really cares about Jonathan,' agreed Coco. 'And kids never regret keeping the Mighty Maker's laws.'

Talking point

The children colour in the green pencil and look at the text: 'Honour your parents'. Draw their attention to the promise in the second part of the verse: 'so that you may live long in the land the Lord your God is giving you.' God knew that if the children of Israel were going to live safely in the promised land they would need to build strong families where children treated their parents with respect. Talk about what the word 'honour' means – and how they can honour their parents today.

Bible base

Exodus 20:12

Prayer

Dear Father, thank you for people who care for us, especially our mums and dads. Help us to love and respect them, and to do what they say. Amen.

7. The Brown Pencil
(No killing)

The next afternoon the toys got a shock. A girl walked into the bedroom – a girl with long red hair and hazel eyes, wearing a green school uniform. Even though Jonathan wasn't there, this girl marched in and made herself at home. She went over to Jonathan's desk and lifted the gold medal he'd won in the 100 metre sprint. And then she did something really weird. She held the medal up to her lips and kissed it.

'She's insane,' Meenie muttered under his breath.

'She's in love, too,' gasped Mo. 'In love with a medal!'

Next minute there was the sound of footsteps on the stairs. The girl tossed her hair back from her face and draped herself round the chair, so she was sitting facing the door, with her chin on her hands, when Jonathan burst into the room.

The boy's jaw dropped when he saw her.

'Kate! Who let you in? Didn't you see the KEEP OUT notice?' he cried.

'Yeah, sure. You want the wrinklies in your life to respect

50

your privacy.' Kate shrugged. 'But I knew it didn't mean me!'

'So what do you want?' Jonathan pushed his glasses up on his nose.

A slow smile spread across the girl's face. 'I need to get today's homework.' She took a packet of toffees from her pocket, unwrapped one, placed it in her mouth and dropped the wrapper on the carpet. 'I missed school this afternoon 'cos I was at the dentist.'

'We've got to write an essay on healthy eating,' said Jonathan. 'Something you know nothing about.'

Kate chewed this over lazily. 'Bet you wouldn't eat healthily either if you lived in the bakery with Mum and me,' she purred. 'Just think. You could have sugar doughnuts for breakfast and chocolate doughnuts for lunch and cream doughnuts for supper. . . mmmm. . . I left some custard ones in the kitchen, by the way.'

'Did you?' Jonathan looked at her more warmly.

The girl unwound herself from the chair and glanced round the room. Her dark-lashed eyes lit on the castle. 'Hello. That king model you gave me – I didn't know it was part of a set.' She darted forward and lifted Eenie and Meenie from the battlements.

'Oh no! She's going to kiss us!' Mo promptly fell over, and the girl picked him up too.

'Can I have these – in return for the doughnuts?' She showed the three figures to Jonathan.

'But why? Why are you so keen on them?' asked Jonathan.

Kate gazed into his eyes. 'Can't you guess?'

'Nope,' Jonathan shrugged.

'I want them because. . .' Kate seemed about to say something and then suddenly changed her mind. 'I want them for cake decorations. My idea is to cut their heads off and stick them on a butter sponge. I think that would look really, really cool!'

Before Jonathan could reply, a shrill little jingle filled the air.

Kate set down the figures. 'Oops! Sorry!' She pulled a mobile phone from her pocket and held it to her ear. 'Oh hi, Mum. . . How are things?. . . What!. . . Turned out bright purple!. . . It hasn't!. . . No, stay where you are. . . I'm coming home. . .' She rang off and gave Jonathan a dazzling smile.

'Mum needs me. Hair problems!' She headed for the door, shedding sweet papers as she went. 'See you soon!' she called back over her shoulder.

'Not if I see you first,' Jonathan muttered grimly.

'I could kill that girl,' he added to himself as Kate slammed the front door.

The figures, meanwhile, were ready to collapse with fright. They couldn't speak, of course, until Jonathan had finished his homework and gone downstairs for tea. But the minute he left their voices rang out in horror.

'How could Jonathan have handed good King Arthur over to that. . . that monster?' gasped Eenie.

'She's going to cut off his head!' groaned Meenie.

'We've got to stop her,' cried Mo.

All evening they racked their brains to think of a plan, but bedtime came and they still didn't have one. Jonathan, though, seemed very pleased with himself. He bounced into the room, licking his lips. 'I ate six custard doughnuts,' he boasted. 'And I don't even feel sick.'

Soon the room was dark and the boy was sound asleep. Nothing could be done to help the king until morning. To pass the time, Maiden China suggested writing another letter.

'Good idea! I'll go and get a pencil,' said Mo.

Mo went out. The figures waited and waited, but he didn't return.

'As if we hadn't enough problems! Now Mo's gone missing,' Maiden China groaned. 'We'd better go and look for him.'

In fact Mo hadn't gone far. The figures spotted him under Jonathan's desk – a small, furtive figure lurking beside the waste-paper basket.

'What are you doing down there, Mo?' called Coco.

'Er. . . clearing up sweet papers,' came the airy reply.

'He has something hidden behind his back,' Minie pointed out.

'Just another piece of rubbish to throw into the waste-paper basket,' said the voice.

'It looks more like one of Jonathan's special pencils to me,' said Maiden China. 'Mo, come back to the cupboard this minute.'

'Now, I want an explanation,' she went on, as a sheepish Mo laid a brown 'Colour with the Commandments' pencil at her feet. 'Why were you trying to get rid of this?'

Mo hung his head. 'I got it out to write our letter,' he muttered. 'But then I read the words "No killing" down the side. And I thought if Jonathan saw that he might change his mind about killing Kate. And I want him to kill her because it will teach her a lesson. She needs to learn not to drop litter and frighten toys.'

'Mo, have you any idea what killing someone really means?' Maiden China asked.

'Well. . . the Cowboys and Indians do it all the time,' said Mo. 'The goodies kill the baddies. And the baddies fall down dead. And then they get up and begin to fight all over again.'

'That's pretend killing, Mo.' Maiden China lifted the pencil. 'In the real world, dead people don't get up again. Once their life is gone, they can't do anything to get it back. And that's why this commandment says that no human should ever kill another. The Mighty Maker, who gives life in the first place, is the only one with the right to take it away.'

'What!' Mo looked shocked. 'I thought killing was a game. Quick! Give me that pencil.' He snatched the 'No killing' pencil from Maiden China. 'I'm going to put this pencil on Jonathan's bed,' he called, as he raced off with it. 'He needs to know the truth about killing.'

'Wait, Mo. Jonathan knows already. He isn't really going to kill Kate. It's just a silly something humans say,' Maiden

China called after him.

But Mo insisted on leaving the brown pencil on Jonathan's duvet.

Dawn had broken by the time he got back to the cupboard. There was only long enough for Maiden China to scribble a quick note to the king and drop it into the school bag before the alarm went off. 'Dear King,' the note said. 'We know you are in danger. But do not fear. We will find a way to rescue you. . .'

Of course, the boy didn't see the tiny piece of paper at the bottom of his school bag, but he did spot the brown pencil on his duvet. 'Hey, how did that get there?' he frowned. Then he noticed the grains of sugar still clinging to the front of his school jumper. 'Ah, I get it.' He brushed the jumper clean. 'Kate must have taken out that pencil to remind me not to kill myself with doughnuts.' Mystery solved, he wiped his sugary hands on the back of his school trousers and returned the brown pencil to the 'Colour with the Commandments' box.

Talking point

After the children have coloured in the brown pencil and looked at the Bible text: 'No killing', talk with them about the things they need to stay alive i.e. food, water, air. These things come from God, but his greatest gift is life itself. If everyone kept God's sixth commandment no one would ever lose their life through murder.

Bible base

Exodus 20:13

Prayer

Dear Father, thank you for the gift of life and all the good things we enjoy. We pray for those who have been hurt through violence. Help people everywhere not to hate and kill, and to remember that all life belongs to you. Amen.

8. The Orange Pencil
(Be faithful in marriage)

When Jonathan went to school, Maiden China gathered up the fallen grains of sugar and got out seven bowls. 'Breakfast is ready.' She set the bowls out on the table in the throne room and divided the sugar between them.

The knights, Coco and Sausage gathered round, but no one felt like eating. They were all thinking the same thing. At any moment Kate might turn their king's head into a cake decoration. The thought was so horrible they couldn't bear to talk about it. So they sat in silence, staring glumly into their bowls. . . until a sudden thud on the cupboard made everyone jump.

Mo ran over to the window.

'It's Micky the monkey!' he cried.

'Tell him to clear off,' shouted Eenie. 'He's a marble-grabbing mischief-maker.'

Mo poked his head out of the window. 'Micky! Eenie says to tell you you're a marble-grabbing mischief-maker.'

'No, no,' spluttered Eenie. 'I said tell him to clear off.'

But it was too late. Micky was already swinging in through the door.

'OK, OK, you listen,' the monkey held up his paws. 'Me here to help rescue your king. Me bring message from sheriff.'

'From who?' said Meenie.

'From sheriff,' Micky repeated. 'You know – he Head Cowboy.'

'This better not be another wind-up, Micky,' warned Maiden China.

'No, most honestly. The message is that sheriff get cowboys in Kate's house to raid Kate's room and rescue king.'

'Are there cowboys in Kate's house?' frowned Coco.

'Me know cowboys all over everywhere,' grinned Micky. 'Cowboys in Kate's house live in the attic.'

'Well it's certainly worth a try!' cried Maiden China. 'Tell the sheriff we'd be glad of his help.'

Micky dipped his finger into one of the bowls on the table and then licked it. 'Sheriff make condition. . .'

Coco rolled his eyes. 'I might have known. So how many marbles does he want?'

'Oh sheriff no care about marbles,' said Micky. 'He got big happy plan. We go outyside and me show you.'

Rather warily, the figures followed the monkey out of the castle. Micky led them to the front edge of the cupboard and gestured around the room. 'Sheriff say life here most boring drag. Same woolly carpet. . . same wooden desk. . . same messy bookcase. . . same lumpy bed. . . So he make big, happy plan to cheer toys up.'

'A concert?' said Coco.

The monkey shook his head. 'No concert.'

'A game of hide and seek?' said Mo.

'No hide and seek,' said Micky. 'Me tell you. Is a wedding.'

'But that's crazy. Jonathan's far too young to get married,' cried Maiden China.

'Oh, Jonathan no bridegroom,' laughed Micky. 'Bridegroom is sheriff's son, Buddy Boy.' And with these words he put two fingers to his mouth and whistled sharply.

Cloppety, cloppety, clop. The figures heard the sound of hoof beats and next thing a beefy young cowboy on a handsome black horse rode out of the cupboard. The cowboy galloped at breakneck speed down the side of the mat, then turned and twirled his lasso above his head before charging towards the cupboard. He reined to a halt directly beneath the spot where the figures stood. 'Howdy Princess. Buddy Boy's the name.' The cowboy raised his ten gallon hat to Maiden China.

'You wave!' hissed Micky.

Maiden China lifted her hand and gave Buddy a limp wave.

The cowboy beamed. 'Ah bet that liddle hand knows a hundred ways ta cook a crumb,' he drawled. 'Now ah'd better get back home for ma lunch. Giddy up, Mushroom!' And away he went.

'Well, you meet bridegroom,' grinned Micky. 'What you think?'

'Er. . . nice horse,' Maiden China nodded. 'So who's the lucky bride?'

'You no work that out yet?' Micky peered at her, brown eyes gleaming.

Maiden China shook her head. 'I haven't the faintest idea.'

'Bride someone you know most closely,' grinned Micky.

Maiden China looked more puzzled than ever. 'Does Jonathan have a doll hidden somewhere?' she whispered to Coco.

'Er no, Your Maidship,' the clown whispered back. 'I think Micky's talking about you.'

'Me?'

'Too right!' Micky clapped his paws. 'Sheriff get cowboy friends to rescue king if most lovely Maiden China say she marry Buddy Boy.'

'You mean she'd be a cowgirl!' cried Eenie.

'And live in the cupboard!' cried Meenie.

Micky nodded. 'Too right. You think. Me call back for answer after lunch.'

The monkey leapt from the cupboard and the figures were left looking at each other in dismay. Nobody knew what to say. One by one they sat down in a circle. After a few minutes Coco went over to the 'Colour with the Commandments' box and came back with an orange pencil. Still without speaking he laid it down in the centre of the circle so everyone could read the words down the side. 'Be faithful in marriage' the pencil said.

In the end, Maiden China said quietly, 'I suppose that means I should marry Buddy Boy.'

Coco frowned. 'I don't think it means that,' he said. 'This commandment is for humans. It's the Mighty Maker telling them that marriage is for keeps. Jonathan's mum and dad got joined together, and so they belong together, like two parts of a set.'

'That's right,' nodded Maiden China.

'But you're already part of a set,' Coco looked round at the knights and Sausage. 'Your maker designed you to be together with a king, four knights, a clown and a dog. This pencil says marriage sets shouldn't be broken up and I say toy sets shouldn't be broken up either.'

'Hear! Hear!' the knights agreed.

'Thank you, Coco, that was very helpful.' Maiden China lifted the pencil. 'I shall write Buddy Boy a letter and ask Micky to pass it on.'

But before Maiden China could put pencil to paper, Buddy Boy himself came riding out of the cupboard. He galloped into the centre of the carpet, stood up in his stirrups and yelled. 'Waal, whadaya say, Princess? Are we gonna get hitched?'

Maiden China shook her head.

'Buddy Boy, I'm made to be part of a set and no good

comes of anyone going against their maker's design,' she called. 'My answer is no.'

Buddy Boy flopped back into his saddle. 'That's bad noos for your king!' he yelled. 'But I ain't cryin. I'll go and git me a sweet liddle ladybird to be ma bride. Giddy up, Mushroom.' He dug his spurs into the horse's flanks and away he rode.

'Well, I'm sure that was the best decision,' Maiden China handed the orange pencil to Coco. 'But we're no nearer to rescuing our king.'

'Too right,' called a cheeky voice. 'But me got most brilliant new rescue plan idea.'

The figures spun round and there was Micky the monkey, waiting for them beside the castle.

Talking point

Many children today are affected by marriage breakdown, either through direct experience or through having a friend whose parents have split up. It is important to be sensitive to this.

Once the children in your group have coloured in the orange 'Be faithful in marriage' pencil, talk about their experience of weddings and other special celebrations. Make the point that when two people marry God's plan is that they should have lots of wedding anniversaries and stay married for keeps. Sometimes, though, things go wrong and the marriage ends in the sadness of divorce. Explain that God still cares and wants to help families when that happens.

Bible base

Exodus 20:14

Prayer

Dear Father, thank you that marriage is part of your good

design for people. Thank you, too, that you are there to comfort families going through the sadness of divorce. Be especially close to the children. Help them to know that their mums and dads still love them and they are not to blame. Amen.

9. The Purple Pencil
(No stealing)

The figures found it hard to believe that Micky really *did* have a brilliant idea to rescue the king, but since they didn't have any ideas of their own they decided they'd hear what the monkey had to say. The trouble was Micky refused to say anything in the castle. 'We go outyside, get fresh air!' He pointed excitedly to the open window above Jonathan's desk. Then he scampered towards it and jumped through, onto the outside ledge. He picked up the gold medal Jonathan had won on sports day as he went. 'You follow! You follow!' Holding the medal between his paws, he tossed the ribbon it hung on back through the window so that it dangled above the desk like a rope. 'Me lift you!' he called.

'He wants to lift us onto the window-ledge.' Maiden China looked worried. 'But I'm sure it's too dangerous. Jonathan isn't even allowed to lean out of the window, never mind sit on the ledge.'

'Please let's go, Maiden China,' begged Mo. 'It would be

great to see the world beyond the bedroom. And if we don't join Micky on the window-ledge we'll never hear his idea for rescuing the king.'

'You hurry. No wastey time.' Micky was jumping up and down with impatience.

The other figures were looking at her so pleadingly, Maiden China felt she couldn't refuse. 'All right. We're coming, Micky,' she called. 'Make sure you don't drop us.'

So one by one the figures tied the green ribbon round their waists. Micky pulled them up to the inside sill and guided them through the open window. Maiden China went first and Coco, with Sausage under one arm, brought up the rear. None of them had ever been outside before. 'I can't believe it!' Maiden China gasped as she stepped out into the sunshine. 'I can see for miles.'

Soon the rest of the figures were beside her, drinking in the view. Directly beneath them was a rambling garden, with clumps of yellow and purple crocuses scattered across the lawn. At the end of the garden, white gates opened onto a tree-lined avenue winding down to a cluster of houses and shops.

'Hey! I know why our house is called Hillside House,' said Mo. 'It's because it's built on the side of a hill.'

'However did you manage to work that out, Mo?' Meenie winked.

'Looky. Kate live there,' Micky pointed a skinny finger at a red-brick bungalow.

'I know! I know!' Mo squeaked excitedly. 'Her house is called Hillbottom House, because it's built at the bottom of a hill.'

The figures stared. So that was the house to which their king had been taken. Maiden China gazed at it longingly. To think King Arthur was behind one of those windows. . . inside one of those rooms. She turned to Micky. 'Please, Micky, tell us your plan.'

'You watch!' grinned the monkey. He held Jonathan's

medal up towards the sun so that sunlight danced on its surface. Then he twisted it, making the light flash. Once. . .
twice. . . three times. 'Is a signal,' he explained. He signalled
again. Flash, flash, flash. . . flash, flash, flash. 'Me send for
Super-Jackdaw.'

And with that – swoosh, plop – a sleek, black bird, with
pale grey eyes landed beside them on the window-ledge.
'Super-Jackdaw at your service,' the bird squawked smoothly.
'How may I help you?'

'Toys here need help to rescue king,' said Micky.

The bird cocked its glossy head to one side. 'A king in need
of rescue, you say. Yes I've had some intelligence on that.
He's being held less than a quarter of a mile away in the home
of the local baker's daughter, I believe.'

'It's that house over there.' Eagerly, Maiden China pointed
to the redbrick bungalow. 'Do you think you can get him
out?'

'No problem, dear lady. Give me the go-ahead, and you'll
have your king home in three pecks of a jackdaw's beak,'
Super-Jackdaw preened. 'Peck One – I tap the window. Peck
two – I get the prisoner onto the ledge. Peck three – I fly in
for a pick-up and airlift him to safety.'

'Oh go ahead, by all means,' cried Maiden China. 'Please
go ahead right away.'

But Super-Jackdaw didn't move. 'There's the little question
of payment, dear lady.' He fixed Maiden China with his steely
eyes. 'Special agents such as I require payment in advance.'

'Payment! But we don't have any money,' Maiden China
gasped.

'Panic not, dear lady. You can pay for my services with
anything that shines. In fact, this little piece of gold will do
nicely.' He pecked at the gold medal in Micky's paw.

'You want medal. Here. You take.' Micky held the medal
out.

'Wait a minute!' Maiden China caught hold of the ribbon.
'That medal belongs to Jonathan.'

At this, Super-Jackdaw's smooth feathers grew ruffled and his eyes gleamed with greed. 'Kyack! I want it.' He snatched the medal and flapped up into the air.

'No!' screamed Maiden China, holding on for all she was worth. Next thing, a desperate tug of war had developed. At one end of the ribbon was Super-Jackdaw, doing his best to make off with the medal and at the other were Maiden China and the rest of the figures, hanging on for dear life. Their combined strength was no match for the jackdaw. Inch by inch they were being dragged towards the edge of the ledge. Who knows what would have happened if Micky hadn't bitten the ribbon in two. But he did, and immediately the figures fell back against the window, while Super-Jackdaw did a somersault in mid-air. 'Kyack! Kyack!' He squawked with shock and the medal fell, glinting and glittering, down into the garden below.

The bird headed for the trees and the figures picked themselves up.

'Me savey day!' grinned Micky.

Maiden China was too tired to argue. She contented herself with giving the monkey a look – the sort of look that let Micky know he'd better not show his face around the castle for a very long time.

Back in the throne room, though, it was herself she blamed most.

'I made a very foolish decision,' she told Coco. 'King Arthur would never have allowed us out onto the window-ledge. We could easily have been smashed.'

'But you did the right thing about the medal, Your Maidship.' Coco produced a purple pencil. 'Look, it says here "No stealing". That means it's wrong to take things that don't belong to you. Like you said, that medal belonged to Jonathan. It wasn't ours to give away.'

'Even so, I'm to blame for losing it,' sighed Maiden China. 'Jonathan will be very upset.'

As she spoke, an excited voice shouted: 'Mum, look what I

found lying on the path!' and a few moments later Jonathan bounded into the bedroom. He made straight for his desk, saw the empty space where his medal had been and cried. 'Hey! I must have found my own medal! How did it get into the garden?' Then he noticed the 'No stealing' pencil which Coco had left beside the box and his astonishment grew.

'There's been some sort of monkey business while I've been out,' he muttered.

Monkey business. How right he was!

Maiden China nudged Coco and smiled.

Talking point

The thought of burglars breaking into their home sometimes worries children – especially at night. If you are aware of this being a problem, take the opportunity to discuss those fears and give reassurance.

Alternatively, after the children have coloured in the purple 'No stealing' pencil, ask them to think of a time when they have been helped by someone's honesty, or share an experience of your own. Point out that most people see the importance of keeping God's 'no stealing' law. Finish by asking children what keeping that law means for them.

Bible base

Exodus 20:15

Prayer

Dear Father, we pray for the police force and for all those who work to prevent crime. Help them to do their job well. Thank you for the many honest people in the world. Help us always to be honest too. Amen.

10. The Grey Pencil
(No lying)

At school on Friday, Jonathan punched a football away from the goal-mouth. Next minute, he was doubled up in pain. 'Oww! It hurts. My wrist hurts!' he yelled.

Jonathan's wrist hurt so much that his teacher thought a bone might be cracked, so she rang Jonathan's mum. Laura Jones was the sort of mother who rarely got into a flap, but she agreed her son's wrist should be checked out at the hospital. There, Jonathan happily drank his way through six fizzy cans from the drinks machine in the waiting-room before getting the all-clear. 'Nothing broken. Just a nasty sprain. Should be right as rain in a week or two,' the doctor said.

A week or two! That seemed ages to Jonathan. He arrived in the bedroom looking tired and cross.

'No cricket. No table tennis. It's a disaster,' he moaned.

'Never mind games,' said his mum. 'What about your schoolwork?'

Jonathan suddenly cheered up. 'No schoolwork either,' he

said. 'I can't write.'

'We'll see about that,' Mrs Jones frowned slightly. For some reason, she always seemed to care more about Jonathan's schoolwork than Jonathan did. She settled the boy comfortably in bed, with his arm on a pillow, and went downstairs. A moment later she was back, looking very pleased with herself. 'I told Dad about your wrist and his boss said you could have an old computer from the office,' she announced. 'Isn't that great! Now your schoolwork won't suffer. You may not be able to write, but you can still press keys.'

'A computer! Wow!' Jonathan beamed. 'Can I have it here in my room?'

'Where would it go? There isn't any space.'

Jonathan looked round and saw what his mum meant. Space was a problem. The only way to fit in a computer would be to get rid of some furniture. He couldn't part with his bed or his desk. The bookcase had to stay, and so did the wardrobe. . . 'I know,' he said, suddenly. 'We could get rid of the toy cupboard. We could have a clear-out and give all my old toys to the church jumble sale.'

'A clear-out!' Mrs Jones' eyes lit up and her fingers started to twitch, as if Jonathan had just pressed a button in her brain. 'That's a great idea. I'll clear the toys out after tea.'

She went downstairs and Jonathan got out of bed and knelt beside the toy cupboard. He used his good arm to fish out some of his old playthings – a Batman, some farm animals, a handful of Cowboys and Indians.

'Goodbye,' he whispered.

Goodbye. The word stabbed Maiden China like a knife. Goodbye. Their days in the bedroom were over.

The boy went to find his mum and Mo burst into tears.

'What's happening? What's happening?' he wailed.

'We're being given to a jumble sale,' said Coco grimly.

'But. . . but. . . we belong here,' sobbed Mo. 'This is where our king will expect to find us. You can't let us be given to a jumble sale, Maiden China. Please, you've got to do something.'

A moment later the seven little figures were huddled round the 'Colour with the Commandments' box. Maiden China lifted out a grey pencil, and studied the words on the side. 'The ninth commandment is "No lying",' she said.

Immediately, Mo dried his eyes. 'Hurrah! That's the answer. We won't be given to the jumble sale as long as we're standing up.'

'Don't be ridiculous, Mo,' said Coco. 'The commandment isn't about not lying down. It's about not telling lies. The Mighty Maker wants humans to be truthful.'

Mo's face fell. 'If not lying down won't save us, what will?' he asked.

Maiden China looked at him sadly. 'I really don't know,' she said.

'Me telly you! Me telly you!' cried a voice. And there was Micky the monkey, as full of bounce as ever. Because he lived on the bed and not in the cupboard, he had no jumble sale worries.

'You savey yourselves by playing most clever trick on Mumsy Jones,' he squeaked. 'Looky see this.' From behind his back he produced the KEEP OUT notice that Jonathan kept hanging on his bedroom door.

'You foldy notice in half like so,' Micky bent the card down the middle. 'Now what that say?' He held up the folded card.

'It says KEEP,' said Mo.

'Too right,' Micky beamed. 'Now you takey KEEP word. And you put word up on top of the castle. Then Mumsy Jones come along. She see KEEP word and she think "Ah, Jonathan want to keepy castle." And she no send you to jumble sale after all.'

The figures looked at each other. 'The idea is that we put the word KEEP on the castle, so Mrs Jones will think it's a message from Jonathan,' said Minie. 'Actually, that might work.'

'Too right,' Micky bounced up and down with enthusiasm. 'Is a super-brilliant idea.'

'Come on then. There's no time to lose,' said Meenie. 'Let's get the notice up onto the battlements straight away.' He took the piece of card from Micky.

'Wait!' cried Maiden China. Her face was pale and the hand in which she held the grey pencil was shaking. 'I can't allow this.'

'But. . . but. . . Your Maidship. . . why not?' stammered Eenie.

'Because it's lying,' said Maiden China. 'Jonathan didn't say he wanted to keep us. He said. . .' her voice wobbled. 'He said "goodbye".' She swallowed. 'And so that's what I'm saying to you now, Micky: "Good-bye". Kindly take your notice and go.'

'You no meany that?' muttered Micky.

'Yes,' said Maiden China firmly. 'I do.'

Tail drooping, the monkey left the cupboard.

'But we *have* to lie. It's our only chance. We'll be thrown out if we don't,' Mo wailed.

'Your Maidship, please,' Coco turned to her, pleadingly. 'Think again.'

Sticking to this decision was the hardest thing Maiden China had ever done. But she remembered King Arthur. She pictured his wise, loving face and deep, kind eyes. 'King Arthur wouldn't have lied, and I'm sure he wouldn't want us to lie either,' she said. Then, without another word, she walked back to the castle.

The rest of the figures followed her in silence. The silence continued as they took their usual positions on the battlements, and all through teatime it hung over the room like a dark thundercloud. Then came the warning rumble of footsteps on the stairs and the storm broke. Laura Jones burst through the door. 'Cleaning frenzy mode' was what Jonathan called it when she marched into the room like that – with her thick, fair hair tied back and a black plastic bag in her hand.

She opened the toy cupboard and cleared out the contents. Batmen, lorries, building bricks, Cowboys and Indians – the black bag kept swallowing them, like a hungry monster, until its shiny tummy bulged. When the cupboard was empty inside, Mrs Jones turned to the top. She put the grey 'No lying' pencil back into the 'Colour with the Commandments' box and moved the box onto Jonathan's desk. Then she lifted the castle.

Click. . . click. . . clatter, the figures all fell over and rolled along the battlements. 'This is it,' thought Maiden China. 'We're about to be swallowed. We'll never see the bedroom again.' But amazingly, they weren't fed to the monster. Mrs Jones didn't throw the castle into the bag. Instead, she set it down carefully on a shelf above Jonathan's desk.

It was the first thing Jonathan noticed when he came back into his room.

'Hey, Mum, what's the castle doing up there on the shelf? Why didn't you give it to the jumble sale?' he cried.

Mrs Jones looked at him oddly. 'Well. . . er. . . that castle is a special handmade toy – the sort of thing people pass on down the family.'

'Pass on down the family?' hooted Jonathan. 'You mean you're keeping it for your *grandchildren*!'

His mother fiddled with a strand of hair that had worked itself loose from her pony-tail. 'Well, yes. . . I mean. . . no. . .'

Jonathan smelt a rat. 'You're hiding something. Go on, tell me the truth. Why *did* you keep it?'

'I *am* telling the truth,' cried Mrs Jones. 'I do want to pass the castle down the family. The fact is. . .'

But before she could say another word, there was a shout from downstairs. 'Hey! I need a hand with this computer.'

Immediately, Jonathan leapt to his feet. 'Dad's home. He's got the computer. Come on! Quick!'

That evening, lying on their sides where they had fallen, the figures heard the sound of things being carried in and other things being carried out. They heard Jonathan chattering excitedly to his dad. They heard bumps and clicks, more discussion, then suddenly a low electronic hum. 'The computer's working,' Jonathan shouted.

'Bedtime,' said his mum.

'Aw. . . ten more minutes. Pleeese. We've only just got it set up.'

The ten minutes stretched to twenty, but finally the figures heard Jonathan settle down for the night. 'Not long, now,' whispered Maiden China. Sure enough, within moments of switching the light off, the boy was out for the count.

'The coast is clear,' said Coco.

But nobody moved. It was as if they all wanted to cling onto the past – to their memories of the bedroom as it had been.

'Come on. We must look.' Reluctantly, Maiden China got up and led the figures to the edge of the shelf.

For one long moment, they looked.

'Oh! Oh! Oh!' Mo's wail broke the silence. It was every bit as bad as they'd feared. Of course they'd expected to see a change, but this was like looking down on a different world. 'It isn't a child's room anymore,' wailed Mo, and for once everyone agreed with him. The old, familiar toy cupboard had gone. And in its place sat a black swivel chair, a split-level desk, and a smart cream computer.

'It's like an office,' said Eenie.

'Or an airport,' said Meenie. 'The toy cupboard has taken off; that cream machine has landed and we've been moved up to the control tower. . . except, of course,' he added, 'we don't control anything.'

'That's not true.' Maiden China shook her head. 'We control something very important. We control ourselves. Super-Jackdaw couldn't make us steal and Micky the monkey couldn't make us lie.'

'But nobody's going to play with us for years and years. We've been stowed away for stupid grandchildren,' growled Minie.

11. The White Pencil
(No coveting)

The figures trooped back into the castle and quickly fell asleep – all except Maiden China. The doll waited until everyone else had dozed off, then she slipped outside and slid down the curtain onto Jonathan's desk.

There she looked round for the pencils. She wanted to write King Arthur another letter. She needed to share the terrible news – to tell him how a cream computer had won Jonathan's heart and taken their place in the bedroom.

'I know the box is here somewhere.' She peered round, remembering how Mrs Jones had moved the pencils from the toy cupboard to the desk. Yes! In the darkness, she could just make out the flat shape of the 'Colour with the Commandments' box beneath the shadowy mushroom of the desk lamp.

Crossing the desk at that time of night was worse than any obstacle course. Maiden China kept bumping into things – first a rubber, then a dictionary – but finally she reached the

74

lamp. She pressed the switch in its base. Hey presto! The light came on and everything seemed less spooky. Maiden China stood in its bright circle. She opened the 'Colour with the Commandments' box with the toe of one dainty foot and feasted her eyes on the pencils. There was a white one, she saw, that Coco had used to stop the fighting the day their king had been taken away. 'No coveting what isn't yours' it said on the side. Maiden China wasn't quite sure what 'coveting' meant, so she slipped back over to the dictionary and looked the word up. She discovered then that coveting meant longing for something you didn't have, and envying whoever had it.

'I suppose we castle figures covet Jonathan's attention and that's why we hate the computer,' she thought sadly. 'But we shouldn't, really. The pencil says it's wrong.'

She lifted the pencil and was just about to begin her letter to the king when she heard a very strange sound – a whirring, clicking, hiccuping sound. She looked up and saw, on the other side of the room, the glowing light of the computer screen. Whirr... whirr... click... click... hiccup... hiccup... the noise went on. Soon the machine was creating such a disturbance that it woke up the castle figures, and brought them sliding down the curtain to join Maiden China on the desk.

'That machine has no consideration for others,' Eenie moaned.

'It makes a worse racket than Jonathan's recorder,' said Meenie.

'We never had this bother with the Cowboys and Indians,' said Minie.

'Hey, Machine! Pipe down, would you?' shouted Mo.

Whirr... whirr... click... click... hiccup... hiccup... The computer ignored them.

While the figures tried to decide what to do next, Micky the monkey bounced onto the desk.

'Is good news,' he announced. 'Computer sick. Computer very, very sick.'

'How do you know that, Micky?' Coco asked.

'Because it write messages on screen and me read them,' announced Micky. 'It say it got most noisy heart disk failure. It say it about to have breakdown.'

'You mean it's going to stop working?'

'Too right,' beamed Micky. 'Is good news, yes? Me want computer to break down most quickly.'

'Hear! Hear!' said Eenie. 'We all hate the computer. It's noisy and it stops Jonathan playing with us. The sooner it breaks down, the sooner he'll take us off the shelf.'

Maiden China sighed and looked down at the white pencil. 'You know that won't happen. Jonathan's growing up. He's bound to prefer computer games to toys. And he's going to be really upset if he gets up tomorrow and the machine isn't working.'

'So what are you saying?' asked Coco.

'If what Micky says is true, and the computer is sick, I'm saying we should try to make it better.'

'You mean fix it?' exclaimed Meenie. 'But how?'

'We won't know how to fix the machine until we find out what's wrong,' said Maiden China. 'Micky, will you carry us over to the computer desk?'

Micky scratched his head and then gave a little bounce. 'OK. Me do deal,' he squeaked. 'Me carry you over to the computer desk. Then tomorrow you invite Micky to castle for most delicious crumb-cake tea.'

'You're invited,' Maiden China nodded. 'Now let's go.'

A few moments later the seven figures stood in front of the computer keyboard.

Whirr. . . whirr. . . click. . . click. . . hiccup. . . hiccup. The machine sounded sicker than ever. Its screen was a most unhealthy shade of green and close up the figures could see why. On the screen was a list of complaints.

WANT MY OWN SECRETARY
WANT TO WORK FOR THE BOSS

DON'T LIKE COMPUTER GAMES
DON'T WANT TO STAY HERE

'Could you believe it!' exclaimed Coco. 'Jonathan got rid of his toys to make room for this computer and here it is, pining away for the office.'

'The ungrateful thing deserves a good poke in the plug,' Minie drew his sword.

'No, no,' Maiden China restrained him. 'We're here to make it better, remember.'

'OK, so how do you fix an unhappy computer?' asked Meenie.

Maiden China thought for a moment. 'By using the keyboard, I suppose,' she said.

'But we can't type!' objected Eenie.

'Yes we can. All we need to do is jump on the keys,' said Maiden China. 'Eenie, you stand on that key over there. Meenie, you go to that key two rows behind him. Minie, I want you to take up position on the fifth key from the left in the front row, with Mo two rows behind you, fifth key from the right. Coco, you stand two keys right of Meenie. And Sausage, there's your key over there, one from Eenie. Each time I call your name, I want you to jump up and down.'

As she spoke the computer seemed to reach desperation point. It stopped hiccuping and let out a long, low moan.

There wasn't a moment to lose.

'Quickly! Into position,' called Maiden China, and the figures raced to their keys.

'Eenie, Meenie, Minie, Mo, Sausage, Coco, Meenie, Sausage.' They jumped in turn as their names were called out.

'Coco,' Maiden China called for a second time. Then she took a running leap across the keyboard and landed squarely on a big key at the end.

Instantly, the moaning stopped. There was a short burst of music and the computer screen changed colour from sickly green to radiant blue.

'Hurrah!' cheered Maiden China. 'It worked.'

'The machine certainly looks and sounds better,' said Coco. 'But what did we do?'

'Well, I knew there was no point trying to reason with a computer,' said Maiden China. 'So we typed in a command. Two words. See if you can guess what they were.'

'I stood on B,' said Eenie.

'I was on E,' said Meenie.

'I jumped on C,' said Minie.'

'I was on O,' said Mo.

'B, E, C, O, N. . . I know. . . I know. . .' barked Sausage. 'We told the machine to BE CONTENT .'

It was getting light when the figures got back to the desk. (They'd had to make the journey on foot because Micky the monkey had been too tired to act as a taxi.) There wasn't time to write the king a letter, so Maiden China handed Mo the white 'No coveting' pencil and asked him to put it straight back into the box.

'Yes, Your Maidship. My pleasure, Your Maidship. Straight away, Your Maidship.' Mo bobbed up and down with delight. 'No covering what isn't yours.' He read the words on the side. 'That's good advice. If you cover things up that don't belong to you, their real owners won't be able to find them.'

'It says "No coveting" not "No covering", Mo,' Coco pointed out.

'But it's still good advice,' said Maiden China quickly. 'The Mighty Maker doesn't want humans making themselves sick and miserable like the computer. Coveting is the opposite to being content.'

'It's hard to be content with life on the shelf,' sighed Coco.

'I'm going to be content,' boasted Mo. 'I'll be content all day today and all day tomorrow. And then, probably, the next day Mrs Jones will have grandchildren.'

'Don't be ridiculous, Mo. That won't happen for years and years. . . not until Jonathan's grown up and has his own children,' said Meenie.

And with that, there was the sound of footsteps in the hall. The figures had only just scurried back up the curtain when Mrs Jones herself came into the room.

For some reason, she'd decided to give Jonathan breakfast in bed. She set a glass of milk and two slices of toast down on the bedside table, and shook the boy gently. 'Wake up, Jon. Wake up. We need to talk.'

Jonathan rubbed his eyes sleepily. 'Mum, it's Saturday,' he moaned. 'We can talk later.'

'I'd rather get this over with.' His mum sat down on the duvet, looking uneasy. 'You. . . er remember yesterday I told you I was keeping the castle to pass on down the family. . .'

'For your grandchildren,' Jonathan yawned. 'I still think that's crazy.'

'Yes, well, the thing is, it really wasn't just my grandchildren I had in mind. You see, you're not going to be an only child much longer, Jon. . .

'What!' Jonathan sat bolt upright. 'You mean. . .'

'I mean,' said Mrs Jones softly, 'you're going to have a little brother or sister.'

Talking point

Colour in the white 'No coveting' pencil. Note how white can be hard to see on the page and say that the word covet can be hard to understand. Ask the children to say what they think the word means. Aim to bring out the idea of wanting something very badly.

Point out that the tenth commandment tells us it is wrong to be jealous and dissatisfied, always wanting things that other people have. It's pointless too, because even if we get what we want, before long we will want something else.

Encourage the children to think or draw pictures of the really important things in their lives (family, home, food, clothes) and to thank God for what he has given them.

Bible base

Exodus 20:17

Prayer

Dear Father, thank you for all the good things you have given us. Help us to be content – and not to make ourselves unhappy by envying others. Amen.

12. The Crown of Gold

Jonathan's mum was expecting a baby! The castle figures almost fell off the shelf in shock when they heard. Jonathan seemed pretty shocked too. 'You're joking!' he gasped. Then he lay back and muttered, 'But I like our family the way it is!'

Mrs Jones spent the next few minutes explaining why the baby was such good news. 'But of course it won't ever take your place, Jon,' she finished. 'We'll love you as much as ever.' Jonathan didn't reply. He lay back on his pillow, with his eyes shut. 'You just need some time to get used to the idea,' Mrs Jones said. And then she went out.

A few moments later, she popped her head round the door. 'I'm off to the church jumble sale. If the phone rings, your dad's in the garden.'

When he was certain his mum had gone, Jonathan got out of bed. He didn't go straight to the computer. He just struggled into his clothes (using his good arm), looking miserable. He was still sitting on the side of the bed when someone came

bounding up the stairs two at a time. 'Hi, Jon. It's me.' The
door sprang open and in burst Kate. Today, her copper hair
was braided into a fountain of tiny plaits, which bounced
around wildly when she moved her head.

'I'm really, really sorry about your arm,' she began. 'I
know you're getting it tough and I don't want to make things
tougher. But there's something you really, really need to
know.' She tossed her braids and took a deep breath. 'It's all
over.'

For a moment, Jonathan thought she was talking about
football. A team from his school were playing another local
school that morning. 'It can't be all over,' he objected. 'The
match didn't start until 9:30. It isn't even half-time.'

'I mean. . .' Kate sat down beside him, braids bouncing.
'It's all over between *us*.'

All over between us! Jonathan looked at her in amazement.
He suddenly felt as if he'd been caught up in a scene from one
of the soaps he sometimes watched on TV. 'All over between
us,' was the sort of thing girlfriends said to boyfriends, or
boyfriends to girlfriends. But he didn't have a girlfriend. He
didn't want a girlfriend. And if ever he did go out with a girl,
that girl certainly wouldn't be Kate. 'Come off it,' he
shrugged.

'I know. This is a blow,' Kate sounded sympathetic.
'You're, like, one in a million, Jon, and I still love you heaps,
only I'm doing ballet and Brownies and French horn and net-
ball and Mum and me, we've just adopted an elephant. So,
like I said, you're a really, really great guy and apart from the
elephant there isn't anyone else, but I've got no time for a
boyfriend. I need space. . .' For a moment she stared at him,
dewy-eyed. Then, delving into the pocket of her jeans, she
whispered. 'Hold out your hand.'

Jonathan immediately whipped his unbandaged arm behind
his back.

'Please. . . I want you to take this,' pleaded Kate. 'It's like
returning an engagement ring. I mean, now that we're

finished, I can't sleep with something you gave me under my pillow any more.'

'I didn't give you anything,' said Jonathan.

'Of course you did, silly. You gave me this king figure. Remember?' And Kate set King Arthur down beside Jonathan on the duvet.

For a moment, Jonathan stared at the little wooden toy. 'That was a swap,' he growled. 'You wanted it for a cake decoration!'

'I wanted it because it was yours,' said Kate. 'I thought you knew that.'

'No,' said Jonathan. 'I hadn't a clue.' He got up and set the little wooden toy on top of the desk.

Kate flashed him a look of admiration. 'You know I think you've taken this really, really well. I mean, it must be pukey for you. . . spraining your wrist and losing a girlfriend. But you've been brilliant. I mean you must be really, really upset, but you're not showing it. Are you upset?'

'Not really,' said Jonathan.

'I understand. You feel numb,' nodded Kate. 'The whole thing has come as a total shock. But you mustn't hide away, or you'll never get over it. You've got to get out. Hey, I know. Come out with me now to the church sale. We'll call in at the bakery on the way and get doughnuts.'

Doughnuts! A hollow feeling in Jonathan's tummy reminded him that it was well over an hour since breakfast. Yes, he nodded slowly – doughnuts definitely sounded like a good idea.

'OK. So what are we waiting for? Come on, then.'

And with that, Jonathan and Kate left the room.

No sooner had they gone than the figures sprang to life. At last! At last! At last! Maiden China was weeping with joy. At last, the dark days were over. Their king had returned.

And there he stood on the 'Colour with the Commandments' box, calm and majestic, with sunlight from the window bathing him in golden light. He cupped his hands to his mouth and called up to the castle: 'Anyone at home?'

Even as he spoke, the knights, Coco and Sausage raced towards the curtains. But Maiden China stayed where she was on the battlements. She allowed herself a few more minutes to feast her eyes on the king – just long enough to see him hug the knights and Coco, and pat Sausage on the head. And then she hurried to the kitchen.

'Aren't you going down to the desk with the others?' asked a passing fly.

'There isn't time,' she said. 'I must brush out the throne room and polish the king's throne and make him a welcome home crumb-cake for tea.'

Meanwhile, down on the desk a solemn ceremony was taking place.

In honour of their loyalty, King Arthur was giving the figures new names.

He began with Sausage. 'From now on, you shall be known as Sausage the Stuck Together.' He bent down and stroked the dog all along his mended back. 'Only those that fall apart know what an achievement it is to stay in one piece.'

The four knights came next.

'Eeenie, the insects told me that you have been a caring older brother to Meenie, Minie and Mo,' the king said. 'From now on, your name will be Eeenie the Elder.'

'Meenie, I heard that you mastered your hurt feelings when the flies misused your name. From now on you will be called Meenie the Mastermind.'

'Minie, I know that you are often tempted to use your sword, but you have not done so – which is a sign of great strength. From now on, you will be known as Minie the Mighty.'

'And Mo. . .' King Arthur paused.

'Yes, Your Majesty,' Mo knelt down at his feet.

'From now on your name will be Mo the Most.'

'I expect that's short for Mo the Most Foolish,' Mo said humbly. 'I've been my usual silly self while you were gone.'

King Arthur smiled. 'On the contrary, dear Mo!' He raised the knight to his feet. 'The Most is short for Mo the Most Loveable.'

Mo beamed. 'Mo the Most Loveable! Oh thank you, Your Majesty. That name makes me glad to be me.'

He skipped back to his place and Coco came forward.

'Dear Coco,' said King Arthur, 'I want to honour you for all the good advice you have given. From today you shall be known as Coco the Counsellor.'

'Hurrah! Hurrah!' The sound of cheering carried up to the castle. It made Maiden China smile as she mixed her crumb-cake. The castle was clean and the cake would soon be ready. She was about to pour the mixture into a thimble when Micky the monkey charged through the door.

'You come! Me takey you!' The monkey wrapped his paws round her waist. 'King Arthur ask to see you most longingly.'

'What!' Maiden China dropped her spoon. She didn't even have time to smooth her apron before Micky swept her away.

And so it was a few moments later that, flushed and with a very creased apron, Maiden China came before the king. By this stage the desk was abuzz with insects and a choir of sparrows had gathered at the window. But Maiden China didn't even notice the spectators.

'Maiden China,' King Arthur was looking at her in delight.

And she looked back. His face seemed more wise and loving than ever, if a little more faded than she remembered.

'Your Majesty,' she curtseyed. 'We have missed you very much.'

'And I, you.' King Arthur took her hand. 'But your thoughtful letters cheered me up. Thank you for all you did while I was gone.'

'It was not me, Your Majesty. It was the words on those pencils.' The doll pointed to the box under the king's feet. 'They helped me to know the difference between right and wrong. But now you have come back to us. And I am glad to return to being the maid.'

A shadow of disappointment crossed the king's face.

'I am sorry to hear you say that,' he said gently. 'For I had hoped you might remain on the throne as my queen.'

The doll gasped. Never had she thought to hear King Arthur say such a thing. To be a queen! His queen! Then she looked over at the 'Colour with the Commandments' box and knew that this could not be.

'Indeed I cannot, Your Majesty,' she said sadly. 'For if the pencils have taught me one thing, it is that we cannot just act as we please. We all know that toys must be what their makers and owners make them. And I was made a servant. As long as I wear this apron, it would be wrong to pretend I'm a queen.'

'She's right,' a small bird chirped from the window-ledge. 'The Mighty Maker made me a sparrow. I can't go round calling myself a hawk.'

'And I was made a spider,' a creaky voice cried. 'It would be wrong for me to call myself a frog.'

There followed a chorus of chirping and buzzing, as all sorts of creatures prided themselves on being what they were. King Arthur was just about to hold up his hand for silence when a thrush suddenly trilled. 'Look out! Look out! Jonathan and Kate are coming up the garden path.'

Jonathan and Kate came cheerfully into the room. Jonathan was carrying a bag of doughnuts, and Kate had a box of paints they'd bought at the sale. From what she said, it was clear to the figures that Jonathan had told her about the baby. 'You're so lucky,' she cooed. 'Babies are brilliant. Plus they're a good source of income. Think of all the stuff you'll be able to buy with the money we get from baby-sitting. Hey! Are you sure you should be doing that?'

Jonathan was removing the bandage from his right arm.

'Course! I'm a quick healer.' The boy cast the bandage aside and flexed his wrist. 'You sort out the paints and I'll get the castle.'

Get the castle? A thrill of excitement passed through the castle figures.

And, sure enough, next minute Jonathan was lifting the castle from the shelf and setting it down beside the king on the desk. 'This castle is for my little brother or sister,' he told Kate. 'The figures just need brightening up to make them good as new.'

The smell of oil paint filled the air. Side by side, Jonathan and Kate worked away happily at the eight castle figures – pausing every now and again to discuss what colour they should paint a cloak or tunic or tail. It was Kate who repainted Maiden China. 'I'm changing her a bit,' she told Jonathan as she worked on the doll's head. 'Like what I've done?' She held up the finished result.

'Sure,' the boy grinned. 'That's it, then. They're all finished. Let's get some lunch.'

Leaving the figures in a row under the desk lamp, Jonathan and Kate went off downstairs.

If they'd lingered for a moment outside the door, they'd have heard a sound like popping corn. It was the figures jumping for joy. 'Look! Look!' Mo the Most raced over to the 'Colour with the Commandments' box. 'We've been painted in all the colours of the pencils. I've got a blue "Have no other gods before me" tunic and red "Have no idols" boots.'

'They gave me black "Respect God's name" spots,' barked Sausage the Stuck Together.

'And I got yellow "Remember the Sabbath day" trousers, green "Honour your parents" socks, brown "No killing" braces and an orange "Be faithful in marriage" nose,' Coco the Counsellor laughed. 'The king has a purple "No stealing" cloak. The knights have grey "No lying" armour. . .'

'And I have a white "No coveting" apron,' Maiden China finished, with a happy smile.

As she spoke, the other figures all turned to look at her. There was a sudden hush, only broken by Mo the Most bursting into tears of delight. 'I'm sorry. It's so wonderful, I can't help it,' he wailed.

'What's wonderful? What are you talking about?' Maiden

China was mystified.

'Minie the Mighty, fetch Her Majesty a mirror,' said the king.

There wasn't a proper mirror on the desk, so the knight fetched Jonathan's medal.

'Her Majesty can see her reflection on the back of this,' he said, kneeling respectfully at the doll's feet.

More mystified than ever, Maiden China gazed into its shiny metal surface. She looked, gasped and looked again, scarcely able to believe her eyes. Then, speechless with joy, she allowed a beaming King Arthur to lead her to the throne room. She was a servant still, but she was also his queen – for Kate had painted a gleaming golden crown around her head.

Talking point

See how many commandments the children can remember and look them up in the Bible. Then draw a circle on a page. Say that God gave these laws to the Israelite people and when they kept them it was like living inside a circle of blessing and safety. The Ten Commandments are important to us too because they remind us that God sets boundaries. There are lots of things we can do, but some things we should not do because doing them takes us outside the safe circle of his will.

Bible base

Exodus 20:1–17

Prayer

Dear Father, thank you that you know what is best for us, your children. Help us day by day to discover your will and make good choices. Amen.

13. From Jonathan's Diary

Months passed. In April, Kate bought Jonathan an Easter egg. In May, Jonathan won another gold medal for running. In June, he helped his mum and dad turn the spare bedroom into a nursery. In July, the whole family went to Devon to visit Great-Aunt Jemima, and in August Kate and her mum sent the Joneses an elephant postcard from Kenya. In September Jonathan went back to school, and started to keep a diary.

The week before his eleventh birthday, the boy wrote about something that had happened that day in class:

MONDAY

We had RE today and Mr Hunter decided to have a quiz. His first question wuz: 'How many commandments did God give Moses?'

Well me being a Bible Brainbox, i knew the answer, so i stuck me paw in the air. 'Yes, Jonathan,' sez Mr H.

'Ten, Sir,' sez me.

Then, all of a sudden Kate calls out, 'Jonathan's got the Ten Commandments on a set of coloured pencils.'

Here, Jonathan stopped writing and glanced over at the 'Colour with the Commandments' box, before returning to his notebook.

If Mr H had been a starving pooch and she'd just given him a T-bone steak, he couldn't have made more of a meal of it. 'On pencils! What a wonderful idea!' sez he. And he starts banging on about how life would be a million times better for everyone if more people kept the commandments. . .

And whaddaya know! Next thing, the girls are all wanting to know where they can get scribblers like mine. Some of the guys sed they wanted them too. So now i've got to ring Great-Aunt Mim. . .

It turned out Aunt Jemima had bought the pencils from a mail-order catalogue. But before Jonathan could do anything more about this, there was a major family event. His mum went into hospital. The baby was on its way.

On Tuesday, after tea, once again Jonathan sat down with his diary. This time the entry was very short.

TUESDAY

Mum went into hospital yesterday and my sister wuz born last night. We're calling her Gemma. Gemma Rose – cos she's pink. Kate sez that's cool.

Jonathan's mum and Gemma came home two days later. Lots of friends from church called in, bringing gifts of baby sleep-suits and chicken casseroles. The postman delivered a small heap of cards, including one from Aunt Jemima. When Jonathan's dad opened the card, it tinkled out a lullaby and a voice sang: 'Be like newborn babes who are thirsty for the pure spiritual milk that will help you grow.' Mr Jones was so surprised he choked on his cornflakes and Jonathan had to thump him on the back. Meanwhile, Mrs Jones was holding up a bib which had fallen out of the card. It had the same Bible verse printed under the picture of the baby on the front. 'That's nice,' she smiled. 'It reminds us we need to drink in God's word to grow spiritually, just the way Gemma needs to drink milk.'

On Friday morning, before Jonathan left for school, the postman delivered a large parcel to the door. The sender's name was clearly written on the wrappings in a neat copper-plate hand: Miss J. Thornberry.

'Aunt Jemima strikes again,' grinned Dad. 'It's for Jonathan this time.'

'She must have sent him a birthday present.' Jonathan's mum looked worried, remembering the hand-knitted woolly jumper that had arrived last year.

But this year Jonathan was really happy with his present. He wrote about it that evening in his diary.

THURSDAY
Well whaddaya know! Today Great-Aunt Mim sent me 28 boxes of 'Colour with the Commandments' scribblers – one for every kid in my class. They came just before I went to school. I took them in and Mr Hunter said Aunt Mim wuz a treasure. Half the class have decided to do the Ten Commandments for their RE project. They're cutting sto-ries from newspapers to show how if more people kept the commandments the world would be a better place.

Jonathan spent Friday evening working on his own gift for Gemma. He was so busy, he didn't get time to write his diary. On Saturday, Kate came over and they worked on the present together. They made progress, but they didn't get it finished. In fact, as Jonathan told his diary, he reckoned they wouldn't get it finished for months.

SATURDAY

Kate came round today. We spent the hole afternoon working on the castle. i am getting it ready to give to Gemma. She won't be able to play with it for a few years, which is good because Kate and me keep finding more things to do. We've moved it down from the shelf onto a table to make room for the greenhouse (made it out of an old goldfish bowl). Now Kate wants to do up the throne room, and i want to make a swimming-pool. By the time we're thru, it will be a masterpiece. . .

As Jonathan was reading out what he had written under his breath, a strange thing happened. He could have sworn he heard cheering from the castle. Rubbing his ears, the boy went over to the coffee table and picked up King Arthur. Funny! The figure's smile seemed broader than before. ZZZZZZZ. A fat bluebottle zoomed excitedly round the battlements. Ah, that explained it. Jonathan returned the king to the throne room. Buzzing, not cheering, was what he'd heard.

The next day was Sunday. On Sunday, as usual, Jonathan went to church – only, of course, this Sunday was different. This Sunday there were four in his family. Being at church with a baby sister gave Jonathan a grown-up feeling, and that evening he tried to put it into words – in between making swipes at the fat bluebottle.

SUNDAY

Feeling groan up. At church today I thort that if my age and Gemma's age were written up as a football score it would be Jonathan – 11 (almost), Gemma - 0.

ZZZZZ ZZZZZZ ZZZZZZZ

Yacked on about growing up spiritually in Bible group. Told Holly, our leader, about getting 'Colour with the Commandments' scribblers for all the kids in my class. She thort that wuz great.

ZZZZZ ZZZZZZZ

> *Holly sez kids grow up stronger and straighter if they
> keep the commandments. But she sez it's trusting Jesus that
> makes uz right with God. She sez Jesus wants to tank uz up
> with so much luv, we'll keep the commandments without
> thinking – which makes sense, i reckon, cos if u really luv
> someone u won't lie to them, steal from them, cheat on them
> or kill them. . .*

ZZZZZZZZ. At this point the bluebottle buzzed right inside
Jonathan's ear. 'Hey! Get off!' He swiped it onto the window,
where it went buzzing furiously up and down the glass.
ZZZZZ ZZZZZ ZZZZZZ.

'Prepare for pulverisation!' The boy raised his arm above
his shoulder. One good swat with his diary should do the
trick. . . and then, just as he was about to slam down the book,
he had second thoughts. Of course he knew the 'No killing'
commandment didn't apply to flies. . . but, why litter the desk
with a squashed bluebottle?

The boy leant forward and opened the window.
ZZZZZZZZZZZZ. The bluebottle soared out into the warm
evening air. . .

And suddenly Jonathan felt as if he was flying with it – flying up over the whitewashed house and the grey stone church
and the redbrick school – flying out into a whole new adven-
ture.

Tomorrow he, Jonathan Jones, would be eleven.

It was the beginning of the rest of his life.

Talking point

Get the children to copy out the Ten Commandments. Then
read the passage from Deuteronomy and ask the children why
they think God would tell the Israelite people to write his laws
and commandments on their gates and door-frames. Help
them see that this encouraged people to keep God's instructions right at the forefront of their minds as they went about

their daily lives. When they did this, their lives went well. Say that for our lives to go well we need to be growing spiritually, and this happens when we think about God's word and keep Jesus and his love at the forefront of our hearts.

Bible base

Deuteronomy 6:1–9

Prayer

Dear Father, thank you for all the teaching and guidance we find in the Bible. Thank you that we can know and follow Jesus. Help us to grow in your love. Amen.

Part Two

CHARACTER-BUILDING STORIES

Rhyming stories on the wisdom of Proverbs

Most of these stories may be used interactively in a group situation. Suggestions for key words and group responses are included with the text. Approximate age range varies – most will work with 6–10-year-olds; stories 17, 19, 23, 24 and 25 are more suited to children aged 9+.

14. King Solomon's Dream
(Put God first)

King Solomon has just been crowned
and now he's in a stew.
As ruler of all Israel
he's not sure what to do.
How will he make decisions?
What if he gets things wrong?
He hasn't much experience.
He still feels very young.

Full of fears and questions,
weighed down by his job,
Solomon makes a sacrifice
– a sacrifice to God.
And that night he has a dream,
– a dream where God appears.
'Ask me for anything,' God says.
'Just ask – and it is yours.'

'Anything!' the king gasps.
He knows God would not lie.
He really can have anything.
How should he reply?
The voice of fortune whispers,
'Ask God for wealth untold.
Ask him to fill your treasure chests
with heaps of shining gold.'

Then he hears the voice of fame
'Ask to be a star.
Ask for a multitude of fans
in countries near and far.'
The voice of victory interrupts,
'Ask God for power and might.
Ask to defeat your enemies
and crush them in the fight.'

But Solomon, he pays no heed
to what these voices say.
Riches, fame and victory
aren't what he seeks today.
He really longs to govern well –
to be both fair and just.
And if he is to do what's right,
then one gift is a must.

This gift is what the new king picks
to help him rule his kingdom.
'Oh God of all the earth,' he prays.
'Give me the gift of wisdom.'
And God delights in this request;
it's pleasing in his eyes.
And so God makes King Solomon
exceptionally wise.

Now Solomon is history –
defunct, departed, dead.
But anyone with a Bible
can read the things he said.
In Proverbs and the Song of Songs,
in Ecclesiastes too,
God still speaks through Solomon.
He speaks to me and you.

Teaching point

When we put God first, he gives us the wisdom to make good decisions and choices.

Bible base

Proverbs 9:10a
'Respect and obey the Lord! This is the beginning of wisdom.' (CEV)
2 Chronicles 1:7–12
(the story of Solomon's choice)

Telling this story

This story can be acted out, with different children playing the parts of Fortune, Fame and Victory. Use a spotlight to represent God, letting it rest on Solomon when he receives the gift of wisdom.

Songs

Seek ye first the Kingdom of God
The wise man built his house upon the rock
Who spoke the words of wisdom and life

15. Bert and the Wolves
(Don't go with the crowd)

You've heard of Little Red Riding Hood
but did you know she'd a brother called Bert?
When Red Riding Hood got her little red cloak
Bert got a red Man U shirt.

You've heard how Red Riding Hood met with a wolf
as she went to her granny's one day.
The wolf raced ahead and hopped into gran's bed
where under the covers it lay.

Red Riding Hood thought the wolf was her gran
till the animal leapt at her throat.
Then the woodcutter came and the wild beast was slain;
still, granny was rather put out.

'I might have a hair on my chin,' she said.
'I might even have two or three.

But that doesn't give Riding Hood any excuse
for mistaking that wolf for me.'

Red Riding Hood's mum tried to put things right.
She could see the old woman was hurt,
so she sent her a cake, and some custard tarts,
and the delivery boy was Bert.

'Take these goodies to granny, Bert dear,' she said.
'Go straight to her house on the green.
Stay out of the wood and steer clear of wolves.
and keep your red Man U shirt clean.'

Well, Bert set off proudly along the path.
It was his first time out all by himself.
There he was, skirting the edge of the wood
when whom should he meet but a wolf.

'Hello, Bert,' said the wolf. 'Goodbye, wolf,' said Bert,
pressing on with a cheerful grin.
He wasn't repeating his sister's mistake.
There'd be no picking flowers for him.

He went on down the path for ten minutes or more,
when out from the wood with a whiz
came a ball, chased by a big hairy wolf
in a red Man U shirt just like his.

'Go on, join in the fun,' said the wolf with a grin.
'You can see you have nothing to fear.
Come into the wood. Meet the rest of the gang.
We're all Man U supporters here.'

'Oh, all right,' said Bert, and he went with the wolf.
But he didn't get much of a game.

For as soon as the wolves saw the young lad appear
they decided to call it half-time.

They gathered around him, licking their lips.
Bert enjoyed the attention and fuss,
so he gave them the cake and the custard tarts
and they said, 'Now you're one of us.'

After eating the food, they rolled in the mud.
Then they went to the woodcutter's house.
'Come on, Bert! Here's a ball. See that window,' they said.
'Bet you can't smash the glass.'

'Bet I can!' laughed Bert. And he kicked the ball
just as hard as he could kick.
It hit the mark. The window smashed,
and suddenly Bert felt sick.

What had he done?
His friends, the wolves, had vanished like rockets in space.
And he was left standing there, covered in mud,
staring into the woodcutter's face.

The woodcutter marched Bert straight home to his mum.
Bert suffered a lot of pain;
and I suppose it wasn't fair really,
for the wolves were also to blame.

But at least our Bert learnt a lesson.
And if you met him, he'd tell you so.
When wolves (or anyone else for that matter) try to get *you* to
do the wrong thing,
always stand firm and say 'no'.

Teaching point

If people try to get you to do wrong, say 'no'.

Bible base

Proverbs 1:10
'When sinners tempt you, my son, don't give in.' (GNB)
Matthew 7:15
'Watch out for false prophets. They come to you in sheep's clothing, but inwardly they are ferocious wolves.'

Telling this story

Divide the children into two groups. Each time you say the words **Red Riding Hood**, group A wave and say: 'Hello' and when you say **Man U shirt**, they chant: 'Un-i-ted'. Each time you say the word **Wolf**, group B growl. When you say the word **Wolves**, everybody howls.

Songs

I've decided to follow Jesus
One more step along the world I go
Though the world has forsaken God
We don't believe the devil's lie

16. Snow White and the Dwarfs
(Be considerate)

Listen up, people! Get your brains in gear.
Snow White and seven dwarfs are our subject here.
This story starts where the fairy tale ends.
Snow White's said goodbye to her seven dwarf friends.
She's settled in the palace, married to the prince.
The dwarfs were at the wedding but they haven't seen her
    since.
'Hey ho!' they say, 'It's time for a vacation.
Let's visit Snow White. We don't need an invitation.'

So, before they go to bed that night,
the dwarfs pen a note to their dear Snow White.
'Snow White,' they say, 'expect us very soon.
We'll be with you on Tuesday or Wednesday afternoon.'
The note is sent and they pack their bags
with socks to be washed and shirts in rags.
Then they set off – hey ho! Hey ho!

104

They step out gladly, marching in a row.

Back in the palace, Snow White can't sleep;
she's got that note and it's made her weep.
'What's wrong, my love?' Her prince appears
and Snow White tells him of her fears.
She loves the dwarfs, but her nerves won't take
them singing in the bathroom before daybreak.
And they always leave dirty socks lying round about.
Having them to stay will wear her out.

Well, the prince is quite a brainy sort of guy
and he tells his Snow White not to cry.
He writes three words on a piece of card
and hangs that sign out in the courtyard.*1
The hours go past. It's near tea-time
when the dwarfs march up in their usual line.
'Hey ho!' they cry. 'Hey ho! Ho hey!
We've come to the palace for a holiday.'

'Not so fast,' says the prince and the dwarfs stop short.
He's blocking the entrance into court.
The seven dwarfs wait and the prince looks wise.
He says, 'Now, friends, here's a surprise –
There are special words which callers must say
before coming into the palace today.
These words, as you see, are hanging on the gate.
BECON is the first, then SIDER, then ATE.
I've hung them there to act as a guide
to everyone who comes inside.'

'But they don't make sense!' the seven dwarfs moan.
'How do we SIDER and BECON?'
The prince gives a smile. He says: 'The trick
is to read those words through very quick. . .'
There's a pause while the dwarfs try to work this out.*2

Then: 'BE CONSIDERATE,' they suddenly shout.

Well, after this talk things can't go wrong.
The dwarfs are considerate all week long.
They help Snow White just as much as they can
and never make a sound before eight a.m.
When, all too soon, they must say goodbye
Snow White thinks she's going to cry.
But before they go she shares something
that makes those seven dwarfs shout and sing.
Hey ho! Hey ho! You should see their grins.
The great news is – she's expecting twins.

Teaching point

God wants us to be considerate of other people.

Bible base

Proverbs 27:14
'You might as well curse your friends as wake them up early
in the morning with a loud greeting.' (GNB)

Telling this story

Get the children to listen out for the word **dwarfs**. Every time
they hear it, they shout: 'Hey ho!' An adult or group of adults
should listen for the word **Snow White**. When they hear it,
they sing: 'Tra la!'

At an appropriate point in the story (see *1) show a sign with
the words BECON, SIDER and ATE set out underneath each
other. Pause at *2 until children work out what the words say.
Then turn the sign round to show the phrase 'Be considerate'.

This story is a good one for Mothering Sunday!

Songs

A new commandment that I give to you
God loves you and I love you
Jesus' hands were kind hands, doing good to all

17. Alfred and the Cakes
(Keep your cool)

The Danes have conquered England. They've plundered far
   and wide.
King Alfred of Wessex is on the losing side.
The Danes have killed his brother, the noble Ethelred.
But Alfred doesn't panic; he's a man who keeps his head.
His forces may be beaten but he plans to fight again
from an isolated island where he camps out with his men.

It's winter on the island. Alfred wants a break
from sleeping under hedges and washing in the lake.
So he calls upon a cowherd, whose home is very plain,
and asks if he might shelter from the wind and from the rain.
Immediately, the cowherd kneels at Alfred's feet.
'Your Majesty,' he stammers. 'You're welcome. Take a seat.'

King Alfred sits beside the fire, feeling rather damp.
His weeks of sleeping rough have left him looking like a tramp.

'Hey, you!' The cowherd's wife appears and shakes her head
   at him.
'I suppose my cowherd husband went and let you in.'
'He did indeed,' says Alfred. 'And now he's gone to fish
for an eel or trout or salmon to make a supper dish.'

The woman shrugs her shoulders. 'Fair enough,' says she.
'If he wants to pamper strangers that's all right with me.'
She turns and rolls her sleeves up. She makes some cakes of
   dough.
She sets them on the open fire where the embers glow.
Then she says it's milking time, and till her return
Alfred is to mind the cakes and see that they don't burn.

King Alfred sits beside the fire, staring at the flames.
Now his mind has drifted from griddle cakes to Danes.
He dreams of winning battles. Meanwhile, the cakes turn
   black.
You could fire them from a canon when the cowherd's wife
   comes back.
The woman looks at Alfred. Briefly, all is still,
Then her rage boils over – angry, loud and shrill.

'I told you to mind them cakes, you maggot of a male!
You let them burn, you idle toad! You crawling cabbage snail!
You're nothing but a donkey – no better than a wart. . .'
'Stop!' a voice behind her cuts the tirade short.
She turns and sees the cowherd, white and quivering.
'Wife!' he quavers. 'Don't you know you're speaking to the
   king?'

At these words two soldiers march into the room.
It seems the woman's outburst has brought about her doom.
But Alfred is a patient man, with loads of common sense.
He brushes off the insults, taking no offence.

'It's true, I burnt the cakes,' he says. 'No wonder she feels cross.'

And he gives the woman money to make up for her loss.

Yes, Alfred was a good king, and victory lay in store.
For he beat the Danes in battle, and forced them to withdraw.
And for many years the Saxons were grateful for the rule
of this wise and godly monarch who never lost his cool.

Teaching point

God can give us the strength to keep calm and ignore insults.

Bible base

Proverbs 12:16
'When a fool is annoyed, he quickly lets it be known. Sensible people will ignore an insult.' (GNB)

Telling this story

Pick out the following words **Danes**, **King**, **Cakes**, **Cowherd**. Each time children hear the word **Danes**, they mime waving spears and shout 'Blue cheese!' When they hear the word **King**, they bow and say 'Bow scrape'. When they hear the word **Cakes** they rub their tummies and say 'Yum yum', and when they hear the word **Cowherd** they mime milking a cow and say 'Moo'.

Songs

Be holy in all that you do
Give me oil in my lamp
Love, joy, peace and patience, kindness

18. Mean Jean
(Help when you can)

Mean Jean
sits smugly at her desk,
working on a project.
She's sure to get a good mark.
Her colouring is perfect.
Her neighbour Grace is colouring too
but her marks won't be high.
How can she colour smoothly when
her felt tips have run dry?
'Can I share your pens?' says Grace to Jean.
Jean gives a tight-lipped frown.
She puts her felt tips in their case
and firmly sets it down.
'Not today,' she shakes her head.
'You always want to borrow.
I don't want to share with you today.
Ask again tomorrow.'

It's lunch-time.
Jean has gone outside
to play with her friend, Sue.
They're giggling, chatting, line-dancing
in a line of two.
Grace looks on with envy
as they hop and turn.
The steps don't look too difficult.
She's sure that she could learn.
'Can I join in?' says Grace to Jean,
'I'll soon get the idea.'
But Jean thinks Grace would spoil things.
Her answer makes that clear.
'Not today,' she shakes her head.
'These steps are hard to follow.
We don't want to dance with you today.
Ask again tomorrow.'

School's over.
Jean has to revise
her spellings for a test.
She gets the work done quickly
then sits down for a rest.
Suddenly the phone rings.
Grace is on the line.
She wants to know the spellings.
She forgot to write them down.
It would only take two minutes
to read Grace out the list
but the show that's come on TV now
is one Jean hates to miss.
'Not today,' she shakes her head.
'I don't want to do this for you.
I've finished with schoolwork today.
Ask again tomorrow.'

It's evening.
Jean is out alone
for her daily jog.
Suddenly, the world goes black.
She's run into thick fog.
She doesn't spot the quarry
till she steps over the edge.
The drop goes down one hundred feet
but Jean lands on a ledge.
There she clings on desperately,
fearing for her life.
'Help! Help!' she yells. 'Help! Help! Help!. . .'
Will anyone hear her voice?

Someone does.
A girl whose day
has all gone badly wrong.
And so she really doesn't feel
like helping anyone.
But Jean's call brings her running
to the quarry face.
'Help! Help!' calls Jean. 'I'm stuck down here.'
'Don't panic,' answers Grace.

Grace unwinds her woolly scarf
and lies flat on the ground.
She lowers the scarf into the pit
and soon Jean's safe and sound.
Still, the girl feels shaken.
What if she'd had to wait
and cling on till tomorrow?
Help then would have been too late.
'Grace,' she says. 'I'm very glad
that, when you heard me shout,
you didn't leave me in that hole
but came and pulled me out.

I'm sure you didn't want to,
but you helped me anyway.
From now on I shall do the same
and help folk out today.'

Teaching point

Help when you can.

Bible base

Proverbs 3:28
'Never tell your neighbours to wait until tomorrow if you can
help them now.' (GNB)

Telling this story

Divide the group in two – Group A clap once each time they
hear the name **Jean**. Group B clap once each time they hear
the name **Grace**.
NB: Before telling this story, check that there isn't a child in
the group called Jean. If there is, change the name of the main
character to **Bean**.

Songs

Love is patient, love is kind
We are one, we are family

19. Plain Jane
(Fight worry with faith)

Tizzle was a demon.
Jane Smith was the human
that Tizzle tried to tempt in different ways.
Tizzle's great ambition
was to win demon promotion
by earning the Head Demon's devilish praise.

TIZZLE: Your Mouldiness, I've tempted my human
successfully for the last twelve months. My
records show 48 fall outs with her best friend,
and 1,691 arguments with her sister.

HEAD DEMON: Yes, yes, I can see you're good at quarrels. But
the girl is far too cheerful for my liking.

TIZZLE: Oh, but I know exactly how to make her
miserable.

HEAD DEMON: Then prove it. Today's Monday. I challenge
you to steal your human's happiness for seven

115

days in a row.

TIZZLE: It will be my pleasure, Your Mouldiness.

Tizzle had a quick look
in his tempter's handbook
to see how he could steal Jane's happiness.
The instructions said that worry
was the answer to his hurry
to cause his human seven days' distress.

At eight o'clock next morning,
without any kind of warning,
Tizzle brought new worries to Jane's thoughts.
He got her in a real state,
whispering she was overweight
and that her face was breaking out in spots.

TIZZLE: You look like Darth Maul on a bad hair
               day
JANE: (to mirror) Oh help! What am I going to do?
TIZZLE: You're going to worry about it. . . go on. . .
               keep worrying. . .

This tactic worked like magic.
Life suddenly seemed tragic.
Jane thought she must have swollen overnight.
At college, all her marks fell.
She simply couldn't work well
because she thought she looked a dreadful sight.

TEACHER: Jane, can you tell me what makes volcanoes
               erupt? Jane. . . Jane. . . I'm speaking to you.
JANE: Oh. . . er. . . sorry, Miss. What did you say?
TIZZLE: She wants to know what has made those spots
               erupt on your forehead.

Jane's misery continued,
as Tizzle planned that it should,
day after day until the weekend came.
He filled her head with insults,
then sniggered at the results,
sure he would achieve his hateful aim.

TIZZLE: Your Mouldiness, I thought I would give you a
               quick progress report. Thanks to me, my
               human has worried non-stop about her
               appearance for the last six days. I left her
               standing on the bathroom scales, planning a
               crash diet.
HEAD DEMON: Well done, Tizzle! Keep this up for another
               twenty-four hours and I'll put you in charge of
               a model agency.

On Sunday, when Jane got up
she felt she couldn't worship;
she had so many worries in her heart.
But her parents said: 'Come on, dear.
We can't leave you at home here.'
So she went along to church to keep them quiet.

And there, during the sermon,
she began to pay attention
as the preacher talked of worries and of fear.
He said the way to beat them
was to use faith as a weapon
and repeat the name the devil hates to hear.

And all at once it hit Jane
that she could call on God's name
in faith, the way this Christian preacher said.
For suddenly she felt sure
that Jesus longed to help her

and calm the constant worries in her head.

JANE (praying):   Father, please help me not to worry about the
                   way I look. I ask this in the name of. . .
TIZZLE: No! Don't say it!! Arghh!

That prayer was like a dagger,
making Tizzle stagger,
for words of faith force demons to retreat.
He gave a wail of sadness
and Jane went home with gladness,
leaving him to languish in defeat.

HEAD DEMON: Ah, there you are, Tizzle. Your human has just
              set off for her friend's house the picture of
              happiness. And now I find you gibbering in a
              corner. Explain yourself!
TIZZLE: She. . . she. . . stopped listening to me. She has
              faith. I didn't stand a chance, Your
              Mouldiness. She called on the name of. . .
HEAD DEMON: No. . . no don't say it.
JANE: Thank you, Jesus! I know you can help me
              beat worry and fear.

Teaching point

God can help us beat our worries and fears.

Bible base

Proverbs 12:25
'Worry can rob you of happiness, but kind words will cheer
you up.' (GNB)

Telling this story

Get the children to act out the bits of dialogue, or pre-record them and insert as required.

Songs

Be bold, be strong, for the Lord your God is with you
Be still and know that I am God
Father I place into Your hands
If I were a butterfly
I'm special because God has loved me

20. Lazy Maisie
(Don't make excuses)

One Monday, at the market, a farmer bought a hen.
The creature's name was Maisie; the farmer's name was Ben.
Ben said: 'I'll house you well, my chuck. I'll give you corn
    and wheat.
I simply ask that you should lay fresh eggs for me to eat.'

On Tuesday, Farmer Ben appeared, with a cheerful cry.
He'd come to pick his egg up, to cook it in a fry.
But Lazy Maisie had prepared a fine excuse for him.
'You can't expect an egg,' she clucked. 'I haven't settled in.'

On Wednesday, Farmer Ben came back, smiling hopefully.
He'd come to pick his egg up, to boil it for his tea.
But Lazy Maisie had prepared a new excuse that day.
'Before you get your egg,' she clucked. 'I need a nest of hay.'

120

On Thursday, Farmer Ben appeared and said without
    preamble,
'It's teatime and I'm hungry. Give me an egg to scramble.'
'Calm yourself!' clucked Maisie. 'I can't work if I'm tense.
This hen-run needs protecting. You ought to build a fence.'

On Friday, when the farmer came, Maisie said at once,
'I know eggxactly why you're here. You want an egg for
    lunch.
But I need entertainment. I've always been that way.
Pipe in some background music, and that will help me lay.'

On Saturday, the bird flew to greet Ben with a squawk.
'Now please don't mention eggs,' she clucked. 'It's time we
    had a talk.
I'm like a woman fearing she's been married for her wealth.
If I'm to work, I need to know you bought me for myself.'

On Sunday, Ben approached the run, clean and smartly
    dressed.
'No eggs,' clucked Maisie quickly. 'Today's a day of rest.'
'That's right, old bird,' the farmer smiled. 'I'm here now just
    for you.
Give me no more eggxcuses, or I'll make you chicken stew.'

Teaching point

God wants us to change lazy habits – not excuse them.

Bible base

Proverbs 22:13
'Lazy people stay at home; they say a lion might get them if
they go outside.' (GNB)

Telling this story

Before telling the story, get the children to make a hen shape with one hand (using fingers to make a beak). Mime squawking (open and shut fingers), pecking (dip the hand) and flapping (move arm in and out). They can then use their hens during the story and mime along when Maisie speaks.

Songs

Be bold, be strong, for the Lord your God is with you
Come on, let's get up and go
Have you got an appetite?
My God is so big, so strong and so mighty

21. The Traveller
(Be fair)

George was a penniless traveller
on a journey across land and sea.
One day, he arrived in a strange little town.
Its name was *Nothing For Free.*

George felt hungry and thirsty
but he couldn't afford to buy bread
so he stood at the door of a baker's shop
and sniffed the fresh loaves instead.

Next thing, Mr Crumb, the Baker,
rushed over and grabbed George's ear.
'Just what do you think you're doing?' he cried.
'You can't smell bread for nothing round here.'

'I'm sorry,' said George. 'I can't pay you.
I'm as poor as the birds in the trees.

I didn't know you charged for smelling your bread.
I beg you, forgive me, please.'

'No excuses!' yelled Crumb, in a temper.
'It isn't my fault that you're poor.
You're coming with me straight to the courts
to be punished for breaking the law.'

Crumb dragged George down to the court-house
where the judge was already in place.
There he sat in his wig and his gown
waiting to hear their case.

'Your Honour,' said Crumb. 'I want justice.
It's important to be tough on crime.
This man stole a sniff of bread from my shop.
He should be jailed for a very long time.'

George didn't know how to argue.
He felt helpless and lost and alone.
'Your Honour,' he cried. 'I'd pay if I could,
but I've nothing to call my own.'

At this the judge took from his pocket
five gleaming coins made of gold.
He put the coins into a little black bag
and gave them to George to hold.

'Now, young man,' he said. 'I want you
to give that purse a good shake.
Let Mr Crumb hear the delightful noise
five clinking gold coins can make.'

Clink. . . clink. . . clink. . . clink the coins rattled
in the black bag George shook to and fro.
He shook it until the judge stopped him and said.

'That's enough. You are free to go.'

Free to go! George couldn't believe it.
Mr Crumb looked shocked and dismayed.
Then the judge stood up, adjusted his wig,
and explained the decision he'd made.

He said: 'At the heart of this problem
lies a smell, for which payment was sought.
In my view, the baker has been paid in full
by the sound he's just heard in this court.

'For it seems to me clear as daylight
that when the sweet smell of bread is sold,
it is right and proper to pay for the scent
with the melodious clinking of gold.'

At these words, Crumb the Baker
stormed off in anger and grief,
while George knelt down at the judge's feet
crying tears of joy and relief.

'Keep the money, my friend,' the judge told him.
'And remember what happened today.
I treated you fairly and did what was right
Go now and act the same way.'

Teaching point

God wants us to treat people fairly, whether they are rich or
poor.

Bible base

Proverbs 21:3
'Do what is right and fair; that pleases the Lord more than

bringing him sacrifices.' (GNB)

Telling this story

Divide the children into three groups. Each time they hear the name **George**, Group A groan wearily; when they hear the name **Crumb**, Group B shout 'Crumpets!' and when they hear the word **judge**, Group C say 'Order!'

Songs

Love is patient, love is kind
Make me a channel of Your peace
One more step along the world I go

22. The Journey
(Be generous)

Joseph set out on a journey.
He'd plenty of gold in his purse.
He'd a cloak on his back and a sword at his side
and he rode a remarkable horse.

Joe called this special horse Marvel.
He really believed she could speak.
But so far she hadn't opened her mouth,
though he'd owned her for over a week.

One day, as Joe trotted quietly
along a green, leafy lane,
a storm blew up, with a flash and a bang,
bringing thunder and lightning and rain.

At the side of the road sat a beggar,
who yelled: 'I'm about to freeze.

The wind has blown my blanket away.
Help me! Oh help me, please!'

Joseph's heart filled with pity,
for the beggar looked haggard and ill,
so he gave him his cloak with its woollen fleece
to keep out the bitter chill.

The beggar took the cloak gladly
and our traveller went on his way
with his gold and his sword, riding Marvel the horse,
who still had nothing to say.

Then into the lane rushed a farmer.
He raced out, with a cry of alarm,
'I've lost all my grain! My children will starve!
Lightning's set fire to my barn!'

Again, Joe was moved to pity.
He knew children need to be fed,
so he gave the farmer his purse full of gold.
'Use this,' he said 'to buy bread.'

Now, it's said troubles never come singly,
and our traveller met three in a row,
for next Joe bumped into a down-hearted lad
whose spade had broken in two.

The lad's job was digging potatoes
but how could he dig with no spade?
'Take this sword,' said Joe. 'It will break up the ground.
Just don't cut yourself on the blade.'

Time passed and Joe journeyed onward,
without sword or gold coins or cloak.
There he was, trotting along the lane

when Marvel, his talking horse, spoke.

'Master,' she said. 'I have watched you
give up your cloak, coins and sword,
and because you have given so generously
you are sure to receive a reward.'

And that night Joe didn't go hungry.
His gold might all have been spent,
but word of his kindness had spread through the land
and folk helped him wherever he went.

Teaching point

Giving brings blessing.

Bible base

Proverbs 11:25
'Be generous, and you will be prosperous. Help others, and
you will be helped.' (GNB)

Telling this story

This story works as a mime.

Songs

Go, tell it on the mountain
God forgave my sin
Make me a channel of Your peace

23. The Blabbermouth
(Don't Gossip)

One day a girl called Tulip
found that her friend Lorraine
was busy sending love poems
to a boy called Wayne.
'You fancy him!' cried Tulip.
 Lorraine's cheeks went red.
'Remember, it's a secret.
Please don't tell,' she said.
'Of course I won't,' said Tulip.
But when her friend had gone
a dreadful, itchy tickle
took over Tulip's tongue.
It waggled here and waggled there.
It told that secret everywhere,
and to everyone.

The next day, Tulip's parents
came up with a scheme
to throw a birthday party
for Tulip's brother, Dean.
They said: 'We'll have a disco
with a band to lead the dance.
But remember, it's a secret.
Don't tell Dean in advance.'
'Of course I won't,' said Tulip.
But before the day was done
that dreadful, itchy tickle
took over Tulip's tongue.
It waggled here and waggled there.
It told that secret everywhere,
and to everyone.

Next morning, Tulip noticed
something rather weird.
When she stuck her tongue out,
it hung down like a beard.
She went straight to the doctor
and told him what was wrong;
'My tongue seems to be growing,
and getting very long.'
'Let's see it,' said the doctor.
'Show me how far it goes.'
So Tulip stuck her tongue out
and it hung down to her toes.

The doctor knit his eyebrows.
Tulip cried: 'Be quick.
Please tell me what's the matter.
Am I very sick?'
'Not really,' said the doctor.
'You've a case of blabbermouth –
a very common problem;

I've seen it north and south.
It's caused by spreading gossip,
blabbing secrets here and there.
Though blabbermouth won't kill you;
it spreads trouble everywhere.'

This was news to Tulip.
Yet the doctor's words rang true.
She walked out of the surgery,
quite clear what she would do.
She went on chatting freely.
She still had lots of fun.
But she cured herself of blabbermouth
by holding back her tongue.
When she heard secrets here and there
she didn't blab them anywhere.
No, not to anyone.

Teaching point

God wants us to use our tongues wisely.
NB: In discussion, bring out the difference between good secrets and bad secrets. Make sure the children understand that they should speak out if anyone is bullying/abusing them. This isn't telling tales and they should not keep it secret.

Bible base

Proverbs 11:13
'A gossip tells everything, but a true friend will keep a secret.' (CEV)

Telling this story

Every time the group hear the word 'tongue', they stick out their tongues and waggle them around.

Songs

Jesus, touch me now
Lord, You put a tongue in my mouth
Who spoke the words of wisdom and life?

24. Goodbye, Mr Bigshot
(Learn to listen)

Mr Bigshot, the headmaster of St Mildred's private school,
was as humpy as a camel and as awkward as a mule.
He never ever listened or cared if he was rude.
He changed his mind from hour to hour, depending on his
    mood.
He terrorised his pupils and drove his staff insane,
snooping round the classrooms, finding reasons to complain.

One day, as Mr Bigshot was snooping in the hall,
a stranger in a waistcoat arrived to pay a call.
'A salesman,' Mr Bigshot thought, with an ugly sneer,
for salesmen often came to school to sell some new idea.
So, instead of listening to what this caller had to say,
Bigshot growled, 'Don't bother me' and walked the other
    way.

Time went on that morning. Bigshot brightened for a while.
Another agent called and he received her with a smile.
She talked of kits with moving parts that kids would love to
  stroke.
But Bigshot hardly listened to a word the woman spoke.
He simply made his mind up to play the generous head.
'Whatever you are selling, I'll take one per class,' he said.

A few days later, Bigshot got a horrible surprise.
The school governors came to see him with fury in their eyes.
They said: 'A millionaire called here to give this school some
  money.
We believe you sent him packing – which really isn't funny.
You didn't listen to him or shake him by the hand.
And now his cheque's been given to St Michael's silver
  band.'

Bigshot huffed and puffed and stammered out an explanation.
He hadn't known the caller wished to make a big donation.
And, even as he babbled, his apology was drowned
by a loud insistent bleating out in the school playground.
And then he heard the woman's voice shouting through the
  door,
'There's a kid for every class out here. Just say if you want
  more.'

He'd ordered goats! Some governors were looking rather sad.
It now seemed crystal clear to them that Bigshot had gone
  mad –
turning down donations, making the place a farm.
They knew that they must act at once to save the school from
  harm.
First, they had to make sure those kid goats were taken back.
And then the greatest goat of all deserved to get the sack.

Goodbye, Mr Bigshot. It's the end of your career.
No longer will you hold St Mildred's in the grip of fear.
Goodbye, Mr Bigshot. We know you did your worst.
Perhaps now, before deciding things, you'll try to listen first.
Goodbye, Mr Bigshot. You haven't left an empty space.
The new head's here. She'll make this school a really happy
    place.

Teaching point

The importance of listening.

Bible base

Proverbs 18:13
'Listen before you answer. If you don't you are being stupid
and insulting.' (GNB)

Telling this story

Divide into two groups. Every time Group A hear the name
Mr Bigshot, they shout, 'Out of my way!' When Group B
hear the word **listen**, they shout, 'Hear! Hear!'

Hold up an illustration of the millionaire in verse 2 and
verse 4, to make it clear what's happening. Similarly, hold up
an illustration of the saleswoman in verse 3 and verse 5.

Songs

Have you seen the pussy cat, sitting on the wall?
I am listening to God
Two little eyes to look to God

25. The Bishop and the Britons
(Take advice)

Germanus was a bishop who sailed across the sea
to land in Ancient Britain in four-two-nine AD.
Soon after his arrival, some Britons came to him
and told him of their troubles, which certainly were grim,
for their enemies, the Saxons, had planned a fierce attack,
and they didn't have the manpower to push those bullies back.

The Britons sounded desperate, full of fear and dread.
'We'll be wiped out in battle by our Saxon foes,' they said.
'Don't panic,' said Germanus. 'We'll pray for God's support.
Take me to the valley where this battle will be fought.'
There, Germanus prayed aloud. His words rang strong and
    clear.
They echoed through the valley and gave him an idea.

He shared it with the Britons. They said: 'That's worth a try.'
So, on three sides of the valley they climbed the mountains high.

137

Down below, the Saxons were churning up the mud,
swarming through the valley, bent on spilling blood.
Then the Britons shot an arrow. It rose and then it fell.
That arrow was their signal to give a mighty yell.

'HALLELUJAH!' came the cry. The Saxon band were
    shocked.
The ground vibrated at their feet. The very mountains rocked.
'HALLELUJAH!' Yet again, the valley seemed to shake.
The sound was like a thunderbolt, making heaven quake.
It echoed and re-echoed, as if to raise the dead.
Terrified, the Saxons took to their heels and fled.

So, thanks to St Germanus and his bright idea,
the Britons saw their enemies scuttle off in fear.
They didn't have to raise an axe or strike a single blow.
They just shouted 'Hallelujah' and watched the bullies go.
And this story has a moral: if we follow God's advice,
he can turn us into tigers – even when we feel like mice.

Teaching point

God wants us to seek his help and advice when we face
problems.

Bible base

Proverbs 20:18
'Get good advice and you will succeed; don't go charging into
battle without a plan.' (GNB)

Telling this story

Divide the children into two groups. When Group A hear the
word **Britons**, they shout: 'Up the Blues!' When Group B
hear the word **Saxons**, they shout: 'Up the Reds!'

Have the word **Hallelujah** printed on a small card. Hold it up each time the word appears in the text. Group B then shout it out at the top of the voices.

This rhyme is loosely based on an historic incident. St Germanus was the Bishop of Auxerre in France. The site of the 'Hallelujah Victory' was Maes Garmon in Flintshire, North Wales, which means 'the field of Germanus'.

Songs

Be bold, be strong, for the Lord your God is with you
I'm too young to march with the infantry
We are warriors

26. Toy Story
(Don't give up)

When Malcolm was a toddler
he had a stroke of luck.
His dad came home from work one day
and gave him Bob the Duck.
Bob Duck was made of plastic.
If pushed down in the bath,
his head came bobbing up again –
and that made Malcolm laugh.

When Malcolm was a little boy
he visited the fair.
His dad went to the hoopla stall
and won a wobbly bear.
Wobbly Bear was legless;
his bottom big and round;
his head, like Bob's, popped up again
if pushed down to the ground.

When Malcolm was a teenager
he planned to make his name
as an artist or musician,
or a writer of great fame.
But no one saw his talent.
No one said he was the best.
He took a hundred lessons
then failed his driving test.

When Malcolm was a student
he thought he was no use.
He dropped out of university
and became a real recluse.
He dozed in bed for hours on end.
Like a creature in its lair,
he lived in murky darkness
and grew a lot of hair.

Then one day the bell rang.
Dad was in the hall.
Malcolm pulled the bedclothes up
not answering his call.
Dad came into the bedroom.
He set a white bag down.
He told the lad to open it
after he had gone.

Dad went – but Malcolm didn't stir.
He wasn't in the mood
for opening mystery parcels
of razor blades or food.
With one toe he poked the bag.
'What's this!' he cried in shock.
He found that bag held two old friends –
Wobbly Bear and Bob the Duck.

He also found a Bible verse
on a card addressed to him.
It said: 'Each time a good man falls,
he rises up again.'
And underneath this proverb
his dad had written a prayer:
'Lord, please make our Malcolm
like his duck and bear.'

Then tears sprang into Malcolm's eyes.
He rolled right out of bed.
He knelt down on the carpet.
'Lord, do it now,' he said.
And as he spoke, the failure
that had crushed him like a weight
was lifted from his shoulders
and Malcolm stood up straight.

When Malcolm was an adult,
he looked back on his life.
'That moment was a turning-point,'
he'd tell Michelle, his wife.
'Good people fall, but rise again,'
he'd tell his own three boys.
Then he'd show them Bob and Wobbly –
two very special toys.

Teaching point

With God's help, we can overcome failures and disappointments.

Bible base

Proverbs 24:16
'No matter how often honest people fall, they always get up
again. . .' (GNB)

Telling this story

This story/poem will work best in an all-age situation. It's a good idea to bring toys similar to Bob and Wobbly as visual aids.

Songs

Come on, let's get up and go
Father I place into Your hands
He who would valiant be
What a friend we have in Jesus

27. *A Human for Christmas*
(Be kind to animals)

The dog family lie in their kennel.
It's Christmas – a time of good cheer.
'A human,' barks two-year-old Rover,
'That's what I want for Christmas this year.'

'A human?' Dad Dog looks doubtful.
Mum Dog growls: 'Humans aren't clean.'
'But all my friends have them,' whines Rover.
'Not giving me one would be mean.'

So Dad Dog runs down to the pet shop.
He says: 'Rover wants someone to lick.
They tell me pet boys are stronger.
But girls are less likely to kick.'

The assistant comes back with a small girl,
saying: 'Susie's the human for you.

She's eight years old and quite brainy.
Already there's lots she can do.'

'Her nose is too long,' complains Dad Dog.
'It sticks out of her face like a beak.
If she's all you've got, though, I'll take her,
as long as you're selling her cheap.'

The assistant hands Susie over.
Then says she needs milk every night
and plenty of fresh fruit and fibre
to keep her hair and eyes bright.

At this, Dad pricks his ears sharply.
'That's enough of your sales talk,' he yaps.
'This human will get our leftovers.
We're planning to feed her on scraps.'

He brings Susie back to the kennel
and there she waits, frozen with fear,
while Rover leaps round, barking madly
and Mum snarls: 'No humans in here.'

That night, Susie sleeps in the garden,
tied up to a post in the shed.
She lies on a floor hard as concrete
for the dogs haven't bought her a bed.

Next morning, her body is aching.
She's hungry and lonely and cold.
Rover keeps trying to tease her
and Mum Dog does nothing but scold.

Poor Susie feels sad and neglected.
'They're so cruel!' She can't help but scream.
The sound of her voice makes her wake up.

Thank goodness! It's all been a dream.

* * *

The Mann family sit round the table.
It's Christmas – a time of good cheer.
'Please Dad,' says eight-year-old Susie.
'Can I have a puppy this year?'

Her dad opens up the newspaper –
He smiles: 'Let's get something well-bred.
A poodle or corgi or spaniel.'
But Susie is shaking her head.

For the dream of having bad owners
is a nightmare the girl can't forget
and it's made her think very carefully
of what they can offer a pet.

She says: 'Lots of dogs are mistreated
and hurt in the cruelest way.
I think we should go to the dog pound
and give a good home to a stray.'

Teaching point

The responsibility of caring for pets.

Bible base

Proverbs 12:10
'Good people take care of their animals, but wicked people
are cruel to theirs.' (GNB)

Telling this story

Divide the children into three groups to play the part of the dog family. Each time **Dad Dog** is mentioned, Group A bark twice. When **Rover** is mentioned, Group B yap excitedly. When **Mum Dog** is mentioned, Group C growl.

Songs

All things bright and beautiful
Have you seen the pussycat sitting on the wall?
Think of a world without any flowers
Who put the colours in the rainbow?

28. *The Three Builders*
(Build wisely)

The tale of the three little pigs
is one you've heard before.
These three pigs built three houses
of brick and wood and straw.
The houses built of wood and straw
were huffed and puffed away.
But the pig who built his house of brick
still lives there today.

This pig became a teacher
in a *sty*lish school,
where he taught every piglet
how not to be a fool.
He also taught these pigs to read
and write and spell and cook,
and once a week he'd open up
a special story-book.

'Now piglets, settle down,' he'd say,
'before I count to ten.
Today I'm going to read you
the tale of three young men.
These three young men were building
their lives as humans do.
Their names were Trample-over,
Tumble-round, and True.

'Trample-over built his life
with silver and with gold.
He aimed to be a billionaire.
He wanted wealth untold.
And so he made his choices.
His architect was his greed.
The life that he designed was built
on other people's need.

'Tumble-round, his brother,
built his life with ease.
He aimed to have a brilliant time –
with just himself to please.
And so he made his choices.
His architect was pleasure.
His life was like a playground
built for hours of leisure.

'Finally, we come to True.
His architect was love.
His life had firm foundations
given from above.
He tried to make good choices.
He was honest, kind and fair.
In every situation
he aimed to build with care.

'And then one day a storm blew up –
the fiercest storm on earth.
It raged around those builders
and took away their breath.
Tumble-round was flattened.
His life came down like straw.
And so did Trample-over's,
despite his wealth galore.'

At this, the pigs would shake their heads.
The room would fill with sighs.
Till Teacher Pig reminded them
that one man had been wise.
'True,' he'd say, 'stayed standing,
through all the swirl and shock.
The bricks with which he'd built his life
made it firm as rock.'

Then Teacher Pig would close the book.
He'd say, 'It's time for break.'
The pigs would leave the story-mat
and give themselves a shake.
They loved to hear that story;
they loved the moral, too.
They felt if they were human
they'd all be wise, like True.

Teaching point

We build our lives wisely when we follow God's design.

Bible base

Proverbs 14:11
'A good person's house will still be standing after an evil-doer's house has been destroyed.' (GNB)

Telling this story

Get the children to listen out for any words to do with building – i.e. brick, built, build, building. Every time they hear one of these words they should stand up and sit down again.

Songs

He who would valiant be
I do not know what lies ahead
The wise man built his house upon the rock

Part Three

COMMITMENT-BUILDING STORIES

Key stories from the life of Jesus

These stories are designed to help children enter into the world of the Bible, employing imaginative detail to bring characters and situations to life. Before telling a story, parents or leaders may wish to point out that we are 'imagining' what it might have been like for different Bible characters to meet Jesus. It is also important that the children should hear/read the actual Bible text.

Where the stories are being used in a group situation, they will work best as a narrative basis for a visual presentation. Children can either mime the action or the narrative could be accompanied by a series of illustrations thrown up on an OHP. If there isn't an artist in your leadership team, you'll find suitable illustrations for these stories in *How to Cheat at Visual Aids* by Pauline Adams and Judith Merrell (Scripture Union, 2001). Approximate age range: 8+.

29. From Heaven to Earth
(The angel's story)

In the turret room of a heavenly mansion a small angel called
Cyril flaps his wings. He's flapping along with an imaginary
orchestra. One long flap. . . two short ones. Boom. . . cha. . .
cha! Boom. . . cha. . . cha! A quick little double flap and
wings banged together. Flickety. . . crash! Flickety. . . crash!
Cyril loves rhythm. One day, he hopes, he'll have his own
drum-kit and add 'oomph' to the heavenly choir.

 After what seems like a few hours, but could have been a
few centuries (time means nothing in heaven), Cyril feels like
some exercise. He jumps out of the window and soars towards
the throne room. Boom. . . cha. . . cha. . . Boom. . . cha. . .
cha. Boom. . . cha. . . cha. . . He's so taken up with his wing-
beat, he forgets to look where he's going. CRASH! He bumps
into a cherub. Their wings get tangled, and next thing they've
landed on top of a grassy hill.

 'Sorry! I didn't see you.' Cyril apologises, feeling silly. The
cherub has just left the throne room and has a very special

glow. How could any angel fail to see a cherub like that?

The cherub's head droops. A small, sparkling tear-drop falls from her cheek. When she looks up, Cyril sees that her blue eyes are brimming. . .

'What's the problem?' he asks, amazed that anyone should shed tears in heaven.

'Earth,' says the cherub.

Earth! Yes, that's true. Earth and the humans who live there are a very big problem. Still, Cyril doesn't see any point in crying about it. As far as he's concerned, earth's a write-off. It's a bit like living in a beautiful garden with a bed of nettles growing outside. He knows earth's there – outside the pearly gates, way down in the stratosphere – and he knows it's a mess. But that's nothing to do with him.

So now he spreads a comforting wing around the cherub. 'There, there. You mustn't upset yourself about earthly pain and death,' he says. 'Humans brought it on themselves. They chose to turn their backs on God and go their own way. The best thing to do is ignore them. . .'

'But. . . but. . . we *can't*!'

'Yes we can,' Cyril interrupts firmly. 'I do.'

'Oh, angel,' a tiny smile creeps across the cherub's tearful face. 'You're in for a shock.'

'A shock? What do you mean – a shock?'

'Hush!' She raises a warning finger to her lips. 'Close your eyes and listen.'

Obediently, Cyril shuts his eyes. Faintly. . . in the distance. . . he hears music – wonderful music. The heavenly choir are rehearsing. The voices of hundreds of basses, tenors, altos and sopranos rise from the streets of gold. Soon, Cyril's wings are tapping. Yes, the heavenly choir has plenty of 'oomph' today. Intricate harmonies. . . rousing crescendos! And what a beat! 'Glo-ry-to God-in-the high-est.' The voices rise in a magnificent climax: 'Peace-to-his peo-ple-on EARTH.'

'What!' Cyril gives a startled flutter. 'Peace to his people on *earth*!' He turns to the cherub. 'What's going on?'

'They're singing about God's rescue plan,' the cherub glows. 'The Father God plans to rescue humans from their misery, so they can share the joy of heaven.'

'But there's no way we can have humans here!' cries Cyril. 'Heaven's perfect and humans are sinful! There's no place for them. They wouldn't fit in.'

The cherub nods. 'That's why God the Son is going to earth,' she says, simply. 'He's going to earth to get rid of their sin.'

'Going to earth!' Cyril repeats after her, struggling to make sense of the words. The Son – God himself – leaving the throne room – going out through the pearly gates – appearing on *earth*. 'But humans could never survive in his presence. One look and they'll shrivel up.'

'The plan takes care of that,' says the cherub. 'The Son will leave his glory behind and become flesh and blood.'

'No!' Cyril staggers backwards. He'd have fallen over if the cherub hadn't grabbed hold of his wing.

'Yes!' she insists. 'The Son will become flesh and blood, so that flesh and blood can receive his Spirit. . .'

As she speaks, there's a blinding convulsion. Light bursts from the throne room. . . pure, searing, holy. In a glorious, breathtaking flash it shoots through the heavenly realm, leaving everything – every tree, every stream, every blade of grass – glowing more brightly.

'Come on!' Still holding Cyril's wing, the cherub tows him, dazed and blinking, from the hilltop. Together, they fly over valleys and rivers, until they're hovering outside the pearly gates.

'Look! Look!' The cherub points down into the darkness below.

Cyril looks. For the very first time since humans cut themselves off from heaven, he looks down on their planet. And what he sees makes him gasp with amazement. The last time he looked, the planet was shrouded in darkness. Now there's a single shaft of light stretching all the way down from the throne room. It's like an outstretched arm – God's arm –

stretched out in love.

With a rush of wings, thousands of angels fly downwards. Down. . . down. . . they flutter, into the skies over Bethlehem. Their joyful voices herald the birth of the Son.

And, with a wave to the cherub, Cyril shoots after them. Down, he plunges – down into the heart of the celestial choir – to give the heavenly chorus all the 'oomph' he can.

'Glory to God in the Highest,' sing the angels.

'And peace. . .' sing the basses.

'And peace. . .' sing the tenors

'And – boom. . . cha. . . cha! Boom. . . cha. . . cha. . . PEACE!' belts out Cyril. 'PEACE to his PEOPLE on EARTH!'

Teaching point

God the Father sent his Son into the world to bring people back to him.

Bible base

Luke 2:8–14

Background information

Angels are spiritual beings, created by God, who help carry out his work on earth. Some things that angels do include bringing messages to people (Luke 1:26), protecting them (Daniel 6:22), guiding them (Genesis 19:16) and fighting against evil (Revelation 20:1–2). Angels are part of the invisible spiritual world around us. Because this world is invisible, we have no way of knowing what heaven is really like, although the Bible does give some pictures. The important thing to remember is that heaven is where God lives. When, by his Spirit, he comes into our lives, heaven begins for us on earth.

Songs

Angels sing
Silent night, holy night
The sky is filled

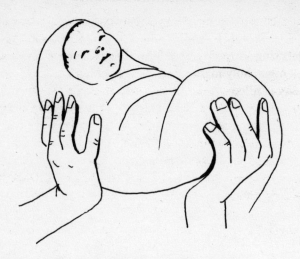

30. The Best Moment of her Life
(Anna's story)

It's early morning in Jerusalem. On a hill overlooking the city stands the magnificent Jewish Temple. The priests have offered the morning sacrifice and already the Temple is busy inside. Teachers of the Law gather in the porches; money-changers open their stalls. In the middle of all this activity, one old woman sits quietly in a corner and prays to God.

The woman's name is Anna and she is a widow. Her husband died just seven years after their marriage. Anna is eighty-four now. She loves God and spends so much time in his house that she almost seems like part of the furniture. People call her a prophetess, for she always seems to be praying. Often, she is so caught up in worship that she doesn't even bother about food.

This morning, she begins her prayers by praising God for his promises. Then, she begins to pray for his chosen people, the Jews. Once, they had been a mighty nation, ruled by their own great kings. But now they are defeated and the Romans are in charge. Tears run down Anna's cheeks as she remembers how little her people seem to care about God. She can see it, even in the Temple. The money-changers are greedy; the priests and Pharisees are proud; worshippers are selfish, and the poor don't stand a chance. These things make Anna sad – but her faith gives her hope. For God has promised in the Scriptures to send a Messiah – a greater king than they have ever had before. 'God, please send your Messiah! Send the Messiah,' she begs.

Because her legs are stiff, the old woman rarely moves from her usual spot. Today, though, she feels God is telling her to get up. She struggles to her feet and hobbles out into the temple court – a small shawled figure amongst the crowd. On her way past one of the stalls, a goat escapes from its tether and almost knocks her to the ground. Somehow, she keeps her balance and shuffles on. She feels sure that there is some reason for God to bring her from her seat.

Suddenly, the crowds part and a space opens up before her. In the space, Anna notices a young mother – scarcely more than a girl – with her husband and baby. There is nothing unusual in that. When Jewish babies are a few weeks old, their parents come to the Temple and make a sacrifice. But beside this little family Anna sees someone she knows – an old man called Simeon. She sees Simeon take the baby into his arms and stare at it with delight. Then he looks up to heaven: 'God, now I have seen what you have done to save your people. I've seen it with my own two eyes,' he cries.

He is talking about the baby. Anna watches him hand the infant back to Mary and Joseph, his parents. She hears him tell them that God will do wonderful things through the child. He also warns the young mother that something will happen in the future that will cause her a lot of pain.

Anna sees the young woman nod, but she does not seem worried. There is no pain now. Only amazement and joy.

For Anna, it's the very best moment of her life. She understands that this baby, called Jesus, is the promised Messiah –

the answer to her prayers. 'Praise God! Praise God!' The old woman takes one last look at the beautiful child, fast asleep in his mother's arms. Then, with the strength and speed of someone half her age, she sets off round the Temple to spread the incredible news.

Teaching point

The birth of Jesus was promised long before it took place. God always keeps his promises.

Bible base

Luke 2:21–38

Background information

Part of God's plan for the world involved choosing the Israelite or Jewish people to get to know him in a special way. He gave them their own land, laws to keep and many promises of blessing. Even though they often did wrong, he kept on loving them. We read the story of God's people in the part of the Bible we call the Old Testament. The promise to send a great king or Messiah is found in Isaiah 9:6–7.

Songs

Come and join our celebration
Come on and celebrate
We believe in God the Father

31. Voice in the Desert
(John's story)

John the Baptist is a man with a message. He lives in the
desert, where all kinds of people from all over the place come
to hear him. There they find a preacher who looks like a
mountain lion. He has a mane of hair on his head; hair on his
face; hair on his brown sinewy arms and legs; even his clothes
are made of camel hair. He looks like a lion and he has a
voice like a lion too – a great, powerful, passionate voice.
And this is his message: 'Turn back to God and be baptised,'
he roars. 'Then your sins will be forgiven.'

The people who take John's message to heart go to the
River Jordan. They wade into this river and John baptises
them. He pushes them right down under the water and then
helps them to their feet. Being baptised like this is a sign that
they are admitting they've done wrong. It is also a sign that
they are sorry and will do their best to change. John tells the
ordinary people to stop being selfish and to share what they
have. He tells tax collectors to stop being dishonest, and not

to collect more tax than is owed. He tells soldiers to stop acting like bullies, and to be content with their pay.

Sometimes the religious experts, known as Pharisees and Sadducees, come to the river. John has an extra loud message for them: 'You bunch of snakes. Do something to show you have really given up your sins,' John roars.

Nobody else dares speak to the Pharisees and Sadducees like that. John doesn't do it because he wants to be rude, but because he's a prophet. God shows him things that other people don't see. John sees that though the Pharisees and Sadducees look good on the outside, they have a lot of pride in their hearts.

There is something else God has shown John – something to do with the future. God has shown him his job is to prepare the way for the promised Messiah. Knowing this, John never wants people to think he is special. 'Someone far more powerful than me is going to come,' he often roars. 'I'm not even good enough to carry his sandals.'

Then one day a man John's own age joins the crowd at the River Jordan. His name is Jesus and he comes from a simple home in Galilee – the home of Joseph, the carpenter, and his wife, Mary. This man wears the plain, white tunic and brown cloak of an ordinary worker. Yet the moment John sets eyes on him his usual message goes right out of his head. His rugged face melts into an expression of wonder. Jesus looks the same as everyone else on the outside, but John sees that his heart is totally pure. Here is someone who is completely right with God.

So when Jesus comes down into the water, all John wants to do is kneel before him. His lion's voice drops to a whisper: 'I shouldn't be baptising you; you should be baptising me.'

Like John, Jesus knows he doesn't need to be baptised. There's no sin spoiling his relationship with God. But baptism is Jesus' way of showing he's truly human.

'Please, you must baptise me,' he insists. 'It's what God wants.'

John gives in when he hears this. Taking a deep breath, he goes over to Jesus' side and does what he has done to so many others before. He pushes Jesus under the surface of the water, and then helps him back to his feet.

Next moment, something amazing happens. As Jesus stands there, with his wet tunic clinging to his body and rivulets of water trickling down his cheeks, God's Spirit comes down from heaven like a white dove and rests on him. 'This is my own dear Son, and I am pleased with him,' God says.

Yes, Jesus is truly human, but he is God's Son, too. And he has the power to put people right with God. Many want to leave sin behind – John's message has seen to that. Now Jesus is about to step out with a brand new message of love – a message that will lead them to freedom.

Teaching point

John made people face the things that were wrong in their lives and he pointed to Jesus – the One who brings believers into a right relationship with God.

Bible base

Matthew 3

Background information

From before his birth, John was set apart for God's service. His mother was called Elizabeth and his father, Zechariah. He was God's appointed messenger (predicted in Isaiah 40:3 and Malachi 4:5) to announce the arrival of Jesus. He fearlessly urged people to turn away from sin. When he urged King Herod to repent of an illegal marriage, he was imprisoned and later killed. At the time of his imprisonment, Jesus sent him a special message of encouragement and said he was the greatest prophet that had ever lived. (Matthew 11:2–14)

Songs

Holy Spirit, fill me now
Jesus, Jesus, holy and anointed one
There is a redeemer

32. The Wedding Feast
(Mary's story)

Until Mary glances at the top table, she thinks the wedding feast is going well. Busy servants scurry about with trays of food. Cheerful guests laugh and chat. It seems a really happy celebration – and then Mary sees the expression on the bridegroom's face. Oh dear! It suddenly strikes her he looks as if he's been spat on by a camel.

Straight away she grabs the tunic of a passing servant. 'What's wrong with your master? He seems worried. Has there been some bad news?'

'You could say that,' Joram, the servant nods. 'Between you, me and this tray of fruit,' he cups his hand round his mouth. 'We've run out of wine.'

Run out of wine! Mary tries not to appear shocked. Running out of food or drink is just about the worst thing that can happen at a wedding. The feast will finish early and people will talk about it for weeks. 'What a let down! That bridegroom couldn't throw a pebble, never mind a

167

party,' the village gossips will sneer.

Thoughtfully, Mary glances over at the table where her son, Jesus, sits. He's set tongues wagging lately, going round teaching about God. 'When's Jesus coming home? Has he given up carpentry for good?' the gossips are demanding. But Mary knows better than to quiz him. Why, she didn't even know if he was coming to the wedding. But there he is, along with some followers, who, like him, seem to have given up their normal work. The woman smiles – sure of one thing. Jesus is, without a doubt, the wisest person in this room. So why not tell him about the wine problem and ask him to help?

A moment later, she is kneeling at her son's side.

'They've run out of wine,' she says simply. She doesn't add, 'and I want you to solve the problem', but that is what she means.

Jesus frowns. Of course, he knows about the wine problem. He also knows that if he solves it, tongues will wag harder than ever. 'Dear woman, you mustn't tell me what to do. My time has not yet come,' he begins. Then his expression changes. Deep in his heart, he hears another voice. The voice of his Heavenly Father telling him to act.

Mary sees the change and imagines he's worked out where to get wine. Eagerly, she beckons to Joram and the other servants. 'Do whatever Jesus tells you,' she instructs them, in case Jesus wants them to make a trip across the village.

But a trip across the village isn't what Jesus has in mind.

Instead, he points to six big stone jars which held the water the guests used to wash before the meal. 'Take those jars and fill them up with water,' he says.

The servants lift the jars and away they go.

Within a few minutes, they stagger back, the jars brimming.

Then Mary hears Jesus tell Joram, 'Now fill your flask from one of the jars. Go up to the top table and give the Master of the Feast a drink.'

What! Mary gasps. This was the last thing she expected. Sending a drink of *water* to such an important guest.

But it's too late to argue. All she can do is watch Joram make his way to the top table and pour some liquid into the important man's cup. Her heart stands still as the well-dressed figure raises the cup to his lips. She watches him sip the liquid, then sniff it, then sip again, then swill it round his mouth. Then he turns and marches towards the bridegroom. At this point Mary shuts her eyes. She can't bear to look. But when she dares to open them, the bridegroom is beaming.

Next minute, Joram rushes up. 'That there water is wine!' he yells. 'And not just any old wine. That there wine is better wine than any we've served all week. I heard the Master of the Feast say so to the bridegroom. And I tasted it myself. It's unbelievable. . . I mean. . .' Suddenly he breaks off, staring at Jesus.

The other servants stare too. And so do Jesus' followers. They are flabbergasted. Jesus has just turned 120 gallons of water into 120 gallons of the finest wine.

'He's worked a miracle,' someone whispers.

'He must be the Messiah,' says someone else.

Jesus doesn't deny it. He simply goes back to his place. 'Nothing's impossible for Jesus.' That's the thought that flashes through Mary's mind. What this means for the future she can only guess. What it means right now is a lot more fun, as the guests sit back and enjoy their miraculous drink.

Teaching point

Miracles seem impossible to us, but God can do the impossible. Jesus' miracles helped people understand that he was God.

Bible base

John 2:1–11

Background information

Wedding feasts in Bible times were lengthy affairs – lasting up to a week. On an arranged evening, the bridegroom would go with his friends to the bride's house. His waiting bride would be dressed in a wedding dress and veil, often with a headband of coins which he had given her. During the wedding ceremony, her veil would be taken off and laid on the bridegroom's shoulder. This was followed by several days of celebration, when many guests would be invited to the home of the bridegroom or his parents.

Songs

My God is so big
O Lord, You're great, You are fabulous
Turn your eyes upon Jesus
Who took fish and bread, hungry people fed?

33. Big Catch – New Job
(Simon's story)

On the shore of Lake Galilee, Simon, his brother Andrew and their fishing partners, James and John, are washing their nets. They have fished all night but caught nothing. 'Ten hours in a boat and nothing to show for it. Who'd be a fisherman!' says Simon, gloomily.

Further along the beach he can see lots of lucky people who don't have to catch fish for a living. He recognises Benjamin, the tent-maker, and Nathan, the potter, amongst the crowd. So why aren't they in their workshops? What has brought so many people to the lakeside?

'What's going on? Why is everybody here?' he calls out to a passer-by.

'We've come to hear Jesus of Nazareth,' is the reply.

'So where is he?' Simon searches the crowd.

'He's over there, heading towards the water,' James points. 'Hey, look, Simon! He's getting into your boat.'

Simon leaps to his feet and pounds across the sand. He runs

heavily, because he's a big man – and he runs fast, because he's strong. Big, strong Simon. Nobody messes with him. And nobody messes with his boat, either. It doesn't matter to Simon that half the population of Galilee seem to be coming to the lake to hear Jesus speak. That doesn't give him the right to take Simon's boat. No, sir! If Jesus thinks he can just make off with Simon's boat, he's another think coming.

Thud! Thud! Thud! At the sound of Simon's footsteps, Jesus looks round at him and smiles. Their eyes meet. Simon has been about to shout, but decides to glare instead. A glare from Simon is usually enough to fluster his opponent. But this time it's Simon who drops his gaze.

'I'd like to borrow your boat. Will you and your brother row it for me?' Jesus asks.

Simon knows he's met his match. No, more than his match. He's met his master.

'The boat's all yours, Master,' he nods.

The reason Jesus needs the boat is so he can speak from it to the crowds. While he speaks, Simon and Andrew keep the boat close enough to the shore for everyone to hear. And, of course, they listen, too. Yes, big, strong Simon, who always expects to do the talking, is hanging onto Jesus' every word. For Jesus has a way of making God real. . . more real than Simon's hunger, more real than his tiredness, more real than the empty nets of the night before.

All too soon the sun is high in the sky, and Jesus needs a break.

'Row the boat out into deep water and let your nets down to catch some fish,' he says.

What! Simon swallows hard. Obviously, Jesus doesn't know much about fishing. Fishermen fish in the shallows in the heat of the day, not in deep water.

'Master, my brother and I worked all night and we didn't catch a sprat,' he bursts out. Then he catches Jesus' eye. 'But if you say so, we'll let the nets down.'

The fishermen row out to where they had been the previous

night and toss the nets over the side. Minutes later, they start pulling the nets in. Simon expects them to come up as quickly and as emptily as they'd done before.

'Ouff!' he grunts in surprise. 'They're heavy.'

'Ouff! They're *very* heavy,' Andrew gasps.

'Quick!' Simon cries. 'Call James and John. We need help.'

What happens next is rather a blur – a very fishy blur. Big fish, medium fish, fish of every shape, size and description – that's what the four fishermen pull out of the lake.

They've started the day with no fish. Now, incredibly, they've landed their greatest ever catch. Awe-struck, Simon kneels down at Jesus' feet.

'Stay away from me!' he mumbles. 'I'm a sinner.'

Jesus smiles. 'Don't be afraid. Today you've brought in fish. From now on you'll bring in people.'

It seems a strange thing to say, but Simon knows what he means. He is asking them to become his disciples – to follow him, learn from him, work with him. Phew! Simon mops his forehead. First the catch of a lifetime. Now the biggest decision of their lives.

By the time they are pulling their boats to the shore, the four friends have made up their minds. They can see that Jesus is full of God's power and they want him for their leader.

'Here! Help yourselves to this fish,' Simon tells the people waiting around.

Then he and James tie up the boats, while John and Andrew spread out the nets.

'Follow me,' says Jesus.

And away with him they go.

Teaching point

While he was on earth, Jesus called ordinary people to be his disciples or followers. He still calls ordinary people to follow him today.

Bible base

Luke 5:1–11

Background information

The setting of this story is Lake Galilee – a big, freshwater lake thirteen miles long and up to seven miles wide. Jesus began his ministry on the shores of this lake. He chose twelve men as his followers or disciples and this story tells how he chose the first four. The main character in the story is a man called Simon. Jesus later changed Simon's name to Peter, meaning 'rock'.

Songs

By blue Galilee Jesus walked of old
I have decided to follow Jesus
I'm a friend of Jesus Christ
I will make you fishers of men

34. In a Stew
(Martha's story)

Martha gets up at dawn. It's going to be a busy day. She's invited Jesus and his disciples to come for a meal. That means 13 hungry men for tea – 14, if you include her brother, Lazarus. As Martha washes and dresses, a picture fills her mind. She sees a table in the courtyard with a spotless white cloth. The table is laden with food: hunks of fresh bread, bowls of figs and olives, a steaming goat stew. It is a real feast – all ready for Jesus to tuck into.

Martha knows that, even with her sister Mary's help, making this happen in real life will take a lot of hard work. She spends the next few minutes drawing up a list of jobs in her head: do washing; grind corn; bake bread; go to market; make stew; lay table. Lazarus, meanwhile, is setting out for the fields. 'Don't forget Jesus is coming for tea. Be home early,' Martha reminds him.

Once Lazarus has gone, Martha tells Mary what's on the menu. 'We'd better get going,' she urges, 'Or we'll never

175

have everything ready in time.' The two women roll up their sleeves. First, they give the big linen tablecloth a really good scrub and spread it out over some bushes to dry. Then they take a bag of corn over to the millstone. While Mary grinds the corn into flour, Martha begins turning the flour into a mountain of dough. They will need a lot of bread to feed so many men. Skilfully, Martha pats the dough into 24 flat cakes, and puts them into the stone oven to bake.

By this stage the sun is high in the sky. 'Now for the stew,' says Martha.

'It's very hot,' sighs Mary. 'Can't we rest in the shade for a while?'

Martha shakes her head. 'No way. We're not making any ordinary old stew, remember. It's for Jesus. I want it to have an extra-special flavour, which means we'll need to gather lots of herbs.'

So they keep going – with Martha ticking the different jobs off her list, each one bringing her closer to her dream of presenting Jesus and the disciples with a really delicious meal.

Mary has a dream too. She dreams of sitting at Jesus' feet, hearing him talk about God. He's such a wonderful teacher – so different from other rabbis; they have no time for women, but Jesus welcomes her questions. He understands her hunger to learn. 'I can't wait for Jesus to arrive,' she murmurs, as they put the stew on to cook. 'There's so much I want to ask him.'

Martha is only half-listening. 'That's right. We need to find out what he wants to drink, and whether he prefers his olives fresh or pickled.' She dips a spoon into the pot on the fire to sample the gravy. 'You know, I think this stew could do with a few more onions. Could you get me a couple from the bunch on the roof?'

A moment later Mary is back, flushed with excitement. 'He's coming! He's coming!' she cries.

'Who? Lazarus?'

'No, Jesus. I saw him while I was up on the roof. He and

the disciples are coming down the street.'

'But he's over an hour early! The meat isn't tender,' gasps Martha, as they run to open the door.

'Jesus! How lovely to see you. Come in! Come in!' Somehow, Martha manages to summon a welcoming smile. 'Take Jesus and the disciples through the courtyard, give them some water to wash their feet, then come back and help me,' she hisses.

'Yes, Martha.' Flushed with pleasure, Mary follows Jesus into the courtyard. She obeys the first of her sister's instructions, but ten minutes later she still hasn't come back.

'What's keeping her?' Martha mutters. 'I can't stir stew, cut up bread and set the table all by myself.'

Five more minutes pass, with no sign of Mary. 'Where is the girl?' Wiping the sweat from her forehead, Martha charges out of the kitchen, only to find her sister sitting happily at Jesus' feet.

'Well, really!' Martha slams a bowl of figs onto the table. Mary doesn't notice, but Jesus looks over and smiles.

That does it. 'Lord,' cries Martha. 'Don't you care that my sister has left me to do all this work by myself? Tell her to come and help me.'

No sooner are the words out of her mouth than Martha feels dreadful. Imagine speaking to Jesus like that! She's dreamt of being the perfect hostess, serving him and his disciples a delicious meal. And now she's ruined everything.

Or has she? Jesus doesn't seem in the least put out. 'Martha! Martha! You're getting all worked up about things that don't matter,' he says. 'Mary's made the best choice. She'll never forget the things I'm telling her.'

He speaks so calmly that Martha calms down too. Leaving Mary to talk, she returns to the kitchen and before long everything is under control. She's dishing up a first-class meal and Jesus is clearly enjoying every bite.

Still, Martha has learnt a lesson – a lesson that has changed her dream. She understands now that her sister made the best choice because she chose to enjoy Jesus' company. So next time Jesus visits, Martha's decided to cook something simple. That way, she'll have more time with him.

Teaching point

Jesus taught his friend, Martha, the importance of spending time with him. How do we spend our time?

Bible base

Luke 10:38–42

Background information

Mary, Martha and Lazarus lived in the village of Bethany on the slope of the Mount of Olives. In a culture where everyone was expected to be hospitable, they went out of their way to make Jesus welcome, and became his good friends. Later, when Lazarus fell sick and died, Jesus raised him from the dead. (See John 11:17–45.) In the days leading up to Jesus' own death on the cross, Mary showed her love for him by pouring expensive perfume on his feet and wiped them with her hair. (See John 12:1–8.)

Songs

Be still and know that I am God
Dear Lord and Father of mankind
Turn your eyes upon Jesus
What a friend we have in Jesus

35. Is She, or Isn't She?
(Jairus' story)

As leader in his local place of worship, Jairus has to make big decisions. He often looks as if he has the cares of the world on his shoulders. Still, there is one person who always brings a smile to his face. 'I'm back, Talitha,' he calls, as he comes home after work. At once, his daughter runs to greet him. The girl is twelve now, but Jairus still uses the pet name Talitha or 'Little Girl' which he gave her when she was small. This slender dark-eyed daughter is Jairus' pride and joy. No matter how tired he feels coming in, the sight of her always chases away his frown.

And then one terrible day, when Jairus calls 'I'm home, Talitha,' Talitha doesn't come. That's enough to tell him that something is wrong – even before he hears his wife's cry: 'Talitha has been taken ill. The doctor's been, but his medicine hasn't helped.'

Jairus races to Talitha's room. He kneels by the bed and takes the sick child's hand. 'Talitha! Talitha!' He strokes her cheek. But there's no response. The girl has stopped smiling. She's stopped talking. She just lies there on the bed, so pale and still that Jairus feels at any moment she may stop breathing too.

Talitha is close to death. Desperately, Jairus cradles her ice-cold hand between his, trying to think what to do. There must be *something*. Yes – suddenly he remembers a piece of news he's heard at work. He springs to his feet.

'Where are you going?' asks his wife.

'Out,' says Jairus. 'I've heard the healer, Jesus of Nazareth is in our area. I'm going to find him.'

Without giving his wife time to object that the religious authorities don't approve of Jesus, Jairus pulls a coat on over his tunic and strides off into the street.

It turns out that Jesus is down at the lakeside. Jairus isn't usually a pushy man, but today he elbows his way desperately through the crowd. And suddenly he's face to face with Jesus. One look into the eyes of the teacher tells Jairus all he needs to know. He sees wisdom. . . strength. . . authority, and he falls to his knees. 'My daughter is about to die. Please come round to my house and touch her so she will get better and live,' he begs.

One look tells Jesus all he needs to know, too. At his feet, he sees a man of faith. A devoted father who hasn't let pride or position stop him coming for help.

But before Jesus can get away from the crowds, some of Jairus' neighbours appear. 'There's no point bringing the teacher round to the house,' they mutter gloomily. 'It's all over. Your daughter is dead.'

Dead. Jairus buries his face in his hands. Then he feels a firm grip on his shoulder. He hears a voice – Jesus' voice – say, 'Don't worry. Trust me.' So that's what Jairus does. Once again, he acts in faith. He doesn't rush home with his neighbours. Instead, he waits for Jesus, hoping against hope. . .

When they finally get back to the house, the place is in uproar. It's the custom when somebody dies for friends, relatives and even strangers to come round and wail loudly. Jairus finds his living-room packed with mourners. Straight away, a group of them gather round him, wailing things like: 'She was such a lovely girl,' and 'You must be heartbroken.'

Before Jairus can reply, Jesus takes over: 'What's all the noise about? The child isn't dead. She's just asleep,' he says.

Asleep! Nobody believes that for a minute. Some folk laugh incredulously, and the mourners wail on. Jesus has a quick word with the three disciples he's brought with him. Next minute, they are ushering the wailers out onto the street.

At last, the house is peaceful.

'Now, take me to your daughter,' Jesus says.

In a daze, Jairus leads the way to the dark-haired figure on the bed. 'She isn't dead, she's asleep,' he keeps telling himself. Still, the sight of his beloved daughter, lying there like a marble statue tears a sob from his throat. She certainly looks dead. But Jesus had said she isn't. So is she, or isn't she? Dumbly, Jairus stands back and Jesus goes over to the bed. Tenderly, he bends over the motionless child. 'Talitha, get up,' he says.

Wham! It's as if the quiet command punches a hole in the stillness of death. Jairus feels it. A jump. . . a jolt. . . a joyful shock of release. Then, before his eyes, Talitha moves. Her cheeks become pink. She sits up. A moment later, she stands up. And next thing she is walking around the room.

'Hurrah! She's alive!' the disciples cheer.

The girl's healing is clearly a wonderful miracle. Just as clearly, though, Jesus doesn't want any fuss. 'Please don't go round talking about this,' he tells Jairus. 'Your daughter is fine. All you need to do now is make sure she has a good meal.' And, with that, he and his disciples slip out of the house.

Jairus and his wife are left trying to act as if nothing out of the ordinary has taken place. Jairus even pretends to worry about work. Even so, Talitha realises something very strange has been going on.

'Who was that man, Daddy?' she asks as she tucks into her vegetable stew.

For a moment, Jairus can't think how to answer. Deep down he believes Jesus is the Messiah. But how can he explain this to his daughter?

Seeing his troubled frown, Talitha comes to his rescue.

'I liked him,' she smiles. 'He reminded me of God.'

And Jairus couldn't agree more.

Teaching point

Jesus healed people when he was on earth. His healing power is still at work in our world.

Bible base

Mark 5:21–43

Background information

Jairus was an important person – a leader or ruler of the Jewish synagogue. His job would have involved looking after the building, supervising worship, running the school on weekdays and finding rabbis to teach on the Sabbath. At that time, many of the religious people – the Pharisees – were suspicious of Jesus. But Jairus did not allow fear of what other people would think stop him going to Jesus for help.

Songs

Go, tell it on the mountain
Jesus' hands were kind hands, doing good to all
Peter and John went to pray

36. Straightened Out
(Zacchaeus' story)

Meet Zacchaeus – a small boy with shifty eyes. He's still at synagogue school, and he's just come to a decision. Zacchaeus has decided to make a career collecting taxes for the Romans. He knows this means other Jews will view him as a traitor. But what has he to lose? He doesn't have any friends, anyway. And tax collectors can make lots of money by getting people to pay more tax than they really owe.

Meet Zacchaeus – fifteen years later – a small man with stony eyes. He's the chief tax collector in the Jericho region. He's also the most crooked, most unpopular man about town. He owns a house with shady courtyards, marble floors, expensive furniture and a bathroom with a sunken bath, but he never has any visitors. No good Jew will have anything to do with him. Zacchaeus' house is known locally as 'The Rathole' and Zacchaeus is known as 'The Rat'.

One day, when Zacchaeus is coming home from a meeting with his Roman masters, he sees a crowd of people have gathered in the street. They're waiting for Jesus. The famous teacher and miracle-worker is expected to reach Jericho very soon.

Zacchaeus has nothing to hurry home for. All that lies ahead of him is a lonely evening, working out who to cheat next and soaking in the bath. So he decides to see what Jesus looks like. There are a couple of problems, though. Being small, he won't see a thing from the back of the crowd, and being hated by everyone, he knows people will happily crush him if he tries to push his way to the front.

Then Zacchaeus spots the answer. A tall, shady sycamore tree. Quickly, the little man tucks the hem of his tunic into his belt. He pulls himself up into a fork in the trunk and starts to climb. And as he climbs, a memory from his schooldays comes flooding back. He remembers how, when the boys in his class were choosing teams, he climbed a tree in the school courtyard to escape the shame of not being picked.

'Jesus! Jesus! Jesus!' The roar of the crowd brings him back to the present. Zacchaeus peers down from his leafy perch and sees that Jesus had arrived. Height is always the first thing Zacchaeus notices about anyone. Jesus isn't tall, he notes, but he looks so full of life and energy he seems to tower over everyone else. All around him, people are jumping and jostling to attract his attention. Jesus strides on purposefully, drawing closer and closer. Then, suddenly, he stops. He stops without warning, directly under the tree.

'Hey, Zacchaeus!' he calls.

Startled, Zacchaeus pokes his head out from between the branches.

'Come down, would you,' says Jesus. 'I'd like to stay at your place.'

What! Is he dreaming? The tax collector blinks and pinches himself. No, Jesus is still standing there, waiting for an answer.

'Stay at my place! Absolutely! You can have a bath if you like!' The little man tumbles joyfully out of the tree.

Meet Zacchaeus, two hours later – a small man with shining eyes. Out of all the Jews in Jericho, Zacchaeus has been picked. He has welcomed Jesus into his home. They've eaten together and talked together. Jesus has laughed at Zacchaeus' jokes and told him a few of his own.

Meanwhile, the local Jews are grouching: 'Jesus must be crazy. Doesn't he know that man is a thief – the greatest little rat of a tax collector that ever lived?'

But when Jesus looks at Zacchaeus, he doesn't see a rat. He sees a miserable, knotted-up human being, who longs to be straightened out.

One evening together – that's all that it takes.

Jesus sits with Zacchaeus and tells him how his life can be different.

'Different.' Slowly, wonderingly, Zacchaeus turns the word over in his head. 'Different. . . different. . . ' And yes, it's true. Thanks to Jesus, he can be different. In fact he *is* different. Suddenly, he leaps to his feet. 'Here and now I'm giving half of what I own to the poor,' he cries. 'And anyone I've cheated will get back four times what I took.'

Meet Zacchaeus, two months later – a big-hearted man with smiling eyes. Yes, really! This is the new Zacchaeus – transformed by Jesus – a true child of God.

Teaching point

Zacchaeus' life was transformed by his meeting with Jesus. Jesus is still in the business of transforming people's lives.

Bible base

Luke 19:1–9

Background information

At the time of Jesus, the land of Palestine was part of the great

Roman Empire. In order to finance their armies and buildings, the Romans forced all the nations they controlled to pay heavy taxes. The Jews especially hated paying these taxes because the money supported a system where people worshipped pagan gods. In their eyes, Jews who collected such taxes were the lowest of the low.

Songs

I was lost but Jesus found me
Nobody liked Zacchaeus
Salvation is found

37. Nadab is Shocked
(The Pharisee's story)

This is a story about a man in flowing robes with a box tied to his forehead. The box holds words of Scripture on small pieces of parchment, and it tells the world the man is a Pharisee.

This Pharisee (we'll call him Nadab) knows everything there is to know about keeping God's Law. 'There are 613 commandments and good Jews must keep every single one of them if they want to please God,' he says. Of course, Nadab knows these 613 commandments off by heart. He understands exactly what they mean and he obeys them to the letter. He never ever works on the Sabbath. He always washes his hands and arms in the proper way before meals, and he gives God a tenth of everything he owns – right down to the herbs in his garden.

Rules. . . rules. . . rules; that's all Nadab cares about. He believes that's all God cares about, too. He has this habit of tapping the box on his forehead, hoping to make anyone who's ever broken a single commandment feel bad.

One day, he even manages to make his brother Pharisees feel bad. It happens at a meeting in Jerusalem. With an accusing tap of his forehead, Nadab brings up the subject of Jesus of Nazareth. 'People from all over the country are flocking to Jesus of Nazareth,' he snaps. 'And we Pharisees sit round doing nothing.'

At this, his brother Pharisees look guilty. Of course, they know about Jesus of Nazareth. For months, reports of things he's been doing in Galilee have been getting back to Jersualem – reports of healings, miracles, changed lives. Some people are even claiming he's the Messiah.

'We can't let more and more people follow someone who doesn't keep our rules,' Nadab fumes. 'You know, he's been going round healing people on the Sabbath.'

Tut! Tut! The Pharisees frown. Their Law allows farmers to rescue animals on the Sabbath, but it doesn't allow healing. No way.

'Nadab is right. We must do something. How about sending a delegation to Galilee to see what is going on?' someone says.

'Agreed,' everyone nods.

'Thank you.' Nadab taps his forehead. 'I suggest we head for Galilee tomorrow.'

So the following day Nadab and Co travel all the way from Jerusalem to Galilee. Throughout the journey, the Pharisee lectures his companions on the ins and outs and ups and downs of keeping the Law. The only time he falls silent is when they pass a ramshackle building.

'Don't your parents live there?' a brother Pharisee asks.

They do, but Nadab won't admit it. This is one subject he doesn't want to discuss. It's a good three months since he last called on his parents. That day the roof had been leaking but Nadab didn't offer to pay for repairs. Instead, he'd given his old mum and dad a lecture about a law which allowed Jews not to support their parents if they were giving extra money to God's house.

Nadab knows he's kept that law. But he doesn't feel like explaining this to his brother Pharisees. So he marches them on past the family home, as if his parents didn't exist.

Eventually, the group reach Galilee. There they find Jesus, teaching by the lake. A ribbon of smoke curls upwards from the wood fire on which the disciples cook. It's a peaceful scene. Within seconds, though, Nadab sees something that shocks him to the soles of his sandals. Before his eyes a couple of Jesus' disciples tuck into a plate of fish. The shocking thing is they don't wash their hands and arms first. 'Look! Do you see what I see?' he explodes. 'Jesus lets his disciples eat without washing.'

'That's dreadful!' The other Pharisees are shocked too. Washing before meals is something every good Jew is expected to do. If they don't, the Pharisees believe the food could contaminate them and make them spiritually unclean.

Like poisonous snakes, Nadab and his companions coil around Jesus. 'Why do you let your disciples eat without washing?' they hiss. Next minute, though, Jesus has turned the tables. He clearly doesn't see anything wrong with his disciples' behaviour. But he does see a lot wrong with his accusers' hearts. Jesus looks at Nadab and sees a proud, selfish man, who knows lots about religion and next-to-nothing about God. 'You disobey God's commands so you can follow your own teachings,' he says. 'For example, God says, "Honour your father and mother", but you have come up with a law that allows children to give no help to their parents. It's that sort of selfishness that makes you unclean – not whether you wash your hands before meals.'

Needless to say, everyone is offended, but Nadab is the most offended of all. In fact, he's so enraged, he marches the Pharisees straight back to Jesusalem for an emergency meeting.

'We now have first-hand evidence to prove Jesus breaks our rules,' one Pharisee begins.

'He's dangerous – very dangerous.' Another agrees.

'So what should we do?' a third Pharisee asks.

Nadab is tapping his forehead. This is the moment he's been waiting for. To Nadab, Jesus is like a pebble – a hateful, irritating pebble rubbing against his pride. 'That's obvious,' he spits. 'We need to get rid of him. We need to get rid of him fast.'

Teaching point

Some people think Christianity is about keeping lots of different rules and regulations, but Jesus taught that the one rule we must follow is the law of love.

Bible base

Mark 7:1–13

Background information

The Pharisees were a strict religious sect who kept closely to God's Law and added lots of extra rules to make sure people did not break it. There were around 6,000 Pharisees at the time of Jesus, and most were opposed to his teaching. Each Pharisee wore a box called a phylactery on his forehead, containing four pieces of parchment with words from Scripture. Another phylactery, containing one piece of parchment, was strapped to the left arm.

Songs

Abba Father
Father God, I wonder
Simple song

38. Hidden Treasure
(The widow's story)

One day, a poor widow gets a wonderful surprise. She wakes up to find that the hens that share her one-room home have laid three brown eggs on the floor. Three eggs! The widow can hardly believe her eyes. One egg is a blessing; two eggs are a great blessing; but three eggs! She feels so thankful, she comes up with a very special plan.

First, she cooks an egg for her breakfast. She doesn't normally eat breakfast, but her plan involves a journey, and she doesn't want to feel dizzy on the road. Next, lifting up the hem of her tunic, she tucks the two remaining eggs into the fold, and carries them carefully across to her neighbour's house.

Rat-a-tat-tat – the poor widow knocks on the door. Her neighbour opens it.

'Oh it's you,' she says, in a not-very-welcoming voice. 'What do you want?'

'Would you like to buy my eggs?' the widow asks.

191

'Not really.' The neighbour gives her an impatient look.

Usually a look like that would make the widow scurry away, but today she stays put.

'They're still warm,' she persists, 'and fresh as the dew.'

'Oh, all right then.' The neighbour takes the eggs and hands the widow two small bronze coins in exchange. They are worth next to nothing, but the widow is delighted. Everything is falling into place.

The second stage of the widow's plan is long and tiring. She has to walk all the way from her village to the Temple in Jerusalem. The road is crowded because lots of other people are heading for the city to celebrate the Passover. But finally the widow reaches the Temple.

There she stops for a moment, almost overcome with wonder and awe. What a magnificent building! The widow has never seen such splendour. Feeling as small as an ant, she follows the crowds up the steps and on through an entrance into a courtyard known as the court of women.

This was where the Temple collection boxes are kept. The widow looks round. With a thrill of excitement, she spots a row of large chests standing upright along the side of the wall. Her plan is almost complete. Today, for once in her life, she has money, and she's reached the part of the Temple where she can give that money to God.

As she fumbles to take out her precious pieces of bronze, a tall merchant in a brightly striped coat pushes past. The widow watches him march up to one of the six collection boxes and drop in a whole bagful of coins. Rattle. . . rattle. . . rattle. They flash and jangle as they fall. The woman marvels. She's never imagined anyone giving God a fortune like that. And then the horrible truth dawns. The people all around her are rich and well-dressed. They are all throwing gold and silver into the chests.

For a moment, the widow wants to run away. 'I shouldn't be here,' she thinks. 'I've got nothing to give in comparison to them.' Yet, deep down, she knows she mustn't let other people stop her carrying out her plan. Her two coins might have no value to those wealthy folk, but she's promised them to God. So she joins the queue. Trying to attract as little attention as possible, she creeps up to one of the chests. Clink. Clink. She slips her coins in, hoping no one will notice they aren't silver or gold.

But somebody does.

Jesus is in the Temple that day. He's come to Jerusalem with his disciples for the Passover celebration. He's been sitting there watching. And now the widow's gift makes him smile with delight. He steps forward and stops her before she can vanish into the crowd.

'Wait a moment,' he says.

Then he calls his disciples and speaks words the widow will treasure for the rest of her life. 'I've seen lots of rich people giving their gifts,' says Jesus. 'But this poor widow put in more than anyone else. All the others have plenty left over to live on, but she's given all that she had.'

Teaching point

The world thinks well of powerful, rich and famous people. But God thinks well of people who make sacrifices for him.

Bible base

Luke 21:1–4

Background information

The two coins which the widow gave were probably Greek coins known as lepta. There were 128 lepta in a silver drachma. One drachma was equivalent in value to a Roman denarius, which was the pay a labourer could expect for a day's work.

Songs

Be bold, be strong
Lord, do I really love You?
Lord, I need Your power

39. What Kind of a King Washes Feet?
(Judas' story)

As one of the twelve disciples, Judas has followed Jesus loyally for the best part of three years. In fact, he acts as treasurer for the group. Not the most honest treasurer, it has to be said. From time to time, Judas has helped himself to money out of the purse, but he sees that as a small reward for his loyalty – a little taster of the BIG reward they are all going to get when Jesus is crowned king.

Judas is looking forward to his reward. That's why he feels so excited when Jesus decides to ride openly into Jerusalem at the beginning of the Passover week. Jesus rides in on a donkey, not on the great white charger Judas would have chosen, but his entry is still a triumph. People gather in their thousands, cheering and throwing down cloaks and leafy branches in his path.

'This is it!' exults Judas. 'All Jesus needs to do now is produce a really great miracle and he'll have the whole city at his feet.'

Only Jesus doesn't produce a great miracle. Instead, as he rides into Jerusalem, he becomes troubled and sad. 'Hey! This isn't fair,' groans Judas. 'This is supposed to be our big moment. We disciples have given up everything. Jesus should be proving we've backed a winner.'

But Jesus doesn't seem prepared to prove anything. Instead, his strange, sad mood continues and Judas feels more and more let down. It's annoying – very annoying. Most annoying of all is the way Jesus keeps talking about death. Of course, Judas knows the religious authorities hate his master and want to take his life. But he also knows Jesus has more power in his little finger than all the priests and Pharisees put together. Plus, he has the crowds on his side. One really big public miracle – that's all it would take to silence his enemies for good.

For some reason though, Jesus holds back. 'A push – that's what he needs,' thinks Judas. 'Jesus needs to be pushed into taking the throne.'

So, two days before the Passover, Judas slips away from the rest of the disciples. He slips away and visits some of the chief priests. 'I know you hate Jesus of Nazareth and want to get rid of him,' he says. 'What will you give me if I hand him over to you?'

The chief priests look at each other. Something about the flat, matter-of-fact way Judas talks tells them he means business. So they make him an offer. Thirty pieces of silver. 'You lead us to Jesus when he's away from the crowds and the money is yours,' they say.

'It's a deal,' nods Judas and off he goes.

Another day passes. It's the evening before the Passover and Judas hasn't quite decided whether to go through with his scheme. That evening Jesus brings him and the other disciples to an upstairs room. There he insists on doing the slave's job of washing everyone's feet. This clinches it for Judas. 'I thought I was following a hero,' he mutters. 'What kind of a king washes feet?'

Soon afterwards, he leaves the house. He makes his way to

the Temple and goes straight to the chief priests' rooms. 'There's an olive orchard called Gethsemane just outside the city,' he tells them. 'Jesus will be there tonight. He'll be alone – apart from his disciples. Just tell your guards to arrest the man I greet with a kiss.'

Word of the plot spreads quickly amongst Jesus' enemies. Within a few hours, Judas finds himself at the head of a small army of guards, religious officials and Roman soldiers. He doesn't feel any shame as he leads that mob to the garden. He doesn't even feel shame as he walks up to Jesus and kisses him on the cheek. In that brief moment, he looks Jesus in the eyes and thinks: 'Go for it, Jesus. Show them your power!'

Poor Judas! To him power means miracles. . . money. . . influence. . . popularity. . . might. He hasn't a clue about God's power – the power of unselfish love. So he kisses Jesus – and there's no turning back. The guards come forward. There's a quick scuffle. One of the disciples cuts off a servant's ear and Jesus immediately heals it. He tells Peter to put down his sword. 'Don't you know I could get my Father to send me twelve armies of angels,' he says calmly. 'But if I did that, what the Scripture says must happen would not be fulfilled.'

What! Judas gasped. Surely his master isn't going to let himself be arrested. No! No! He can't. He mustn't. And yet there he is, standing quite still as the guards yank his hands behind his back and tie them with a rope. 'Hurrah! Hurrah! Kill him!' the crowd jeer.

And this is when the shame bursts upon Judas – a wave of shame so strong, it sends him rushing from the garden. He didn't mean this to happen. No matter. He's to blame. Thanks to him, the King of Love is being treated like a criminal. For thirty pieces of silver he's betrayed his Lord.

Teaching point

Jesus always used his power unselfishly for other people's

good. He calls his followers to serve others unselfishly too.

Bible base

Matthew 21:1–11, Matthew 26:1–56

Background information

The Passover was one of the most important Jewish festivals. It took place in the Jewish month of Nisan (around the beginning of April). On that night, every Jewish family sacrificed a lamb as a reminder of the first Passover back in Egypt, when the angel of death had passed over the Israelite homes which had blood sprinkled on their doors. (See Exodus 11–12.) The Passover was always held in the home, but by New Testament times many people flocked to Jerusalem for the celebration. Visitors would often hire rooms where they could eat the Passover meal with their families.

Songs

Ho, ho, ho, hosanna
Hosanna, hosanna
We want to see Jesus lifted high

40. Execution Day
(The centurion's story)

It's Friday. Execution day. Pontius Pilate, the Roman governor, has given the order and Jesus of Nazareth is to be crucified. The centurion in charge of executions smiles grimly as he puts on his armour. So much for fairness! Jesus may not be an enemy of Rome, but he'll be executed along with two thieves, just the same.

As the sun rises, the centurion orders his men to plant three upright posts – one for each criminal – on top of a skull-shaped hill. Golgotha, the place is called. The centurion feels uneasy as he inspects its grassy slopes. He isn't looking forward to this execution. Putting men to death doesn't bother him, but today's execution spells trouble. After all, Jesus is a well-known figure, and when well-known figures are crucified, crowds can get out of hand.

Back in the city, the centurion prepares to escort the prisoners to the place of execution – and here he hits his first problem. He must parade the prisoners through the city streets, carrying their crossbeams. But Jesus has already been tortured and beaten that morning. Even to a hardened soldier, his appearance is shocking. Blood-soaked hair. . . swollen lips. He's in no fit state to carry a heavy plank of wood. How, the centurion wonders, will he get this man all the way to Golgotha?

Sure enough, half-way to Golgotha, Jesus falls on the road and can't get up. Anxious to keep things moving, the centurion collars the nearest bystander. 'Hey you! What's your name?'

'Simon – Simon of Cyrene.'

'Well, Simon, we've a prisoner here who's too weak to carry his cross. We need you to carry it for him.'

Thanks to this quick-thinking, the centurion has everyone on the hilltop by 9.00 a.m. The next challenge is getting the prisoners nailed to their crosses. The more they struggle, the longer it takes. Today though, the soldiers get through the whole messy business in record time. They hang Jesus on the centre cross, with a thief on either side. The two thieves writhe and curse as the nails go in, but Jesus doesn't resist. He doesn't even groan as they hoist him up onto the upright post and drive a final spike through his feet.

So far so good. Still, the centurion has problems. Just as he'd feared, there's trouble from the crowd. The religious Jews don't like the sign over Jesus' head: 'This is Jesus – the King of the Jews', it says. Of course, the centurion can see why they don't want anyone to think the weak, powerless man under the sign is their king. But orders are orders. He can't go changing the words without permission.

So the sign stays put, fuelling the Jews' hatred. They go out of their way to show how much they despise Jesus. They insult him, mock him, taunt him. And their hatred is infectious. The soldiers, the passers-by, and even the two thieves join in. 'Save yourself! If you're really the Son of God, come down from the cross,' passers-by yell. 'Some king! He saved others, but he can't save himself,' the religious leaders jeer.

Jesus doesn't answer them.

The morning wears on, and the centurion only hears him

speak twice. Once, he gasps out a prayer, 'Father, forgive them, for they don't know what they're doing.' Then, a while later, he asks one of the forlorn band of followers near the cross to look after his mother.

In spite of himself, the centurion is moved. If Jesus had groaned and cursed, he could have ignored him. But there's real power in his silence. 'I'm not in control – he is.' That's the thought that flashes into the soldier's mind. He tries to fight it. . . but it keeps coming back.

And then, suddenly, one of the thieves has a change of heart. He, too, has felt the spiritual power of this broken man. 'Lord, remember me when you come into your kingdom,' he calls. And for a third time the centurion hears words of love from Jesus' swollen lips: 'Today you'll be with me in paradise.'

By now it is midday. The sun should be blazing down from a clear, blue sky. Instead, the light is fading. The centurion looks up, only to see the day cloak itself in blackness, leaving the hillside shadowy and cold.

He shivers. Years of training keep him outwardly calm. Inside, though, he's wretched. Ashamed of his job. Ashamed of himself. Orders are orders, but this execution is plain wrong. Anyone can see Jesus isn't a criminal. 'He's a good man,' the centurion tells himself. 'A very good man. He doesn't deserve to be crucified.'

And it's true. Jesus doesn't deserve to die – let alone in this terrible way. The centurion knows it. The angels know it. The devil himself knows it. Jesus doesn't deserve death because he's lived every single second of every single minute of every single day in loving obedience to God. What this means, though, is that he is the one person who can save sinners. . . the one person who can take their punishment and die in their place. So now, on the cross, he battles on – praying for the world he is dying to save. The hours ahead will be the longest, hardest, loneliest hours anyone will ever endure. Yet Jesus is willing. . .

For three more hours he hangs there.

Then, at last, he gives a great shout. The earth shakes. There are moments of panic and confusion. 'He's dead,' someone cries.

Dead. At the foot of the cross, the centurion trembles with amazement and fear. He doesn't understand what has happened. He's no way of knowing the mighty effect of the Saviour's death. But he's seen how Jesus died and he knows, beyond doubt, that this was no ordinary man.

'Surely he was the Son of God,' he says.

Teaching point

When Jesus died on the cross, he took the punishment for human sin.

Bible base

Matthew 27:32–54, Isaiah 53:1–8

Background information

Crucifixion was a Roman form of punishment. It was especially cruel because criminals could take days to die. In Jerusalem, the high priest and the Jewish council, called the 'Sanhedrin' were in charge of local affairs, but they didn't have the power to order crucifixion – only the Roman governor could do that. That was why the Jewish authorities went to Pontius Pilate and persuaded him to put Jesus to death. A centurion was a Roman soldier who had charge of 100 men.

Songs

Jesus' love is very wonderful
Thank You for the cross
You laid aside Your majesty

41. Why – What – How - Where?
(Mary Magdalene's story)

Jesus is dead. Mary Magdalene has watched him die. She's
been one of a small group of women huddled by the cross.
She's heard him cry: 'It is finished!' She's felt the whole earth
shake beneath her feet. Before her eyes a Roman soldier has
plunged a spear deep into Jesus' side. She's seen the blood
flow from his lifeless body. It's all over. Jesus – her beloved
master – is dead.

Mary is left with all sorts of questions. 'Why' questions
mostly. Why did Jesus die? Why did they kill him? Why did
God let it happen? But there are 'what' questions, too. What
does this mean? What will become of her? And – most
urgently – what will happen to his body?

The answer to this question brings Mary a tiny scrap of
comfort. Usually corpses are left on their crosses for the birds
to pick the flesh from their bones. But tomorrow is the
Sabbath. The Jews want everything over and done with before
their Holy Day begins. So the Roman Governor has allowed a

man called Joseph of Arimathea to bury Jesus. Nicodemus, another secret disciple, is there to help.

The heartbroken women watch the two men take Jesus' body from the cross. Joseph wraps it in fresh linen and Nicodemus sprinkles in the spices he has brought. Because the Sabbath begins at sunset, they have to work quickly. Too quickly, Mary thinks. Sorrowfully, she and the other women follow Joseph and Nicodemus into a nearby garden and see Jesus laid to rest in a cave-like tomb. The men roll a large stone across the door and the women make their plans – plans to prepare their own perfumes and spices – to bring them to the tomb on Sunday and anoint the body themselves.

The thought of doing this one last thing for Jesus helps Mary through the next dreadful day. As dawn breaks on Sunday morning she's up, preparing her spices. Then she joins her friends and they make their way back to the tomb.

And as they walk, they talk a little. Of course, nobody asks the huge 'why' questions. No, they stick to the practical 'how' questions – how, for example, are they going to get into the tomb? The Pharisees have told the Roman governor that Jesus' disciples might try to steal his body.

'He's had the tomb sealed and guarded. I hope we'll be able to move the stone,' Mary sighs.

As it turns out, the women get into the tomb, no problem. The stone has been rolled away, and there isn't a guard in sight. But no sooner do they go in than Mary gives a cry of dismay. 'His body! Where's Jesus' body?' Sure enough, the body isn't there. Mary sees a cocoon of linen grave-clothes sitting on the low stone shelf. But the cocoon is hollow. The tomb is empty. Jesus' body has disappeared.

So now the 'how' questions become one big 'where' question. Where has the body gone? Mary fears the worst. 'The Romans or the Pharisees must have taken it,' she moans. 'Perhaps they've put it on display, or tossed it into a criminal's grave.'

And, next thing, she's running. She's left the tomb and

she's running back into the city to tell the disciples, Peter and John, the terrible news. 'They've taken the Lord's body and we don't know where they've put it,' she gasps.

Immediately, the two men head for the garden. Mary tries to keep up with them, but she's out of breath already and soon gets left behind. By the time she reaches the tomb, the place is deserted. She sees no sign of the disciples. No sign of the other women.

At this point, tears are streaming down Mary's face. She is desperate to find Jesus' body. 'Please let it be here. . . please let it be here.' Sobbing her heart out, she looks inside the tomb and sees two angels, one seated at the top and one at the bottom of the place where the body had been. Angels! Of course, most people would be shocked to see angels, but Mary has been through so much lately, the shimmering figures scarcely make her blink.

'Woman, why are you crying?' the angels ask.

'They have taken my Lord away and I don't know where they have put him.'

She turns from the angels and hears the same words.

'Woman, why are you crying?' This time the speaker is a man. Mary's sobs have dulled her hearing and blurred her vision. She thinks the figure is the gardener – someone who might know where Jesus' body is – who might even have taken it himself. 'Sir,' she sobs, 'if you have carried him away, tell me where you have put him and I will get him.'

'Mary, ' he says.

Mary knows that voice. There's only one person who says her name like that.

'Master!' she gasps. Yes – it's him! Jesus is standing there in front of her. The tomb is empty – not because his body has been taken, but because God has brought him back to life.

'Don't hold onto me,' he tells her gently. 'I am about to return to my Father.' In other words, he can only stay for a few moments – just long enough to turn Mary's sorrow into an indescribable joy.

Bubbling with happiness, the woman leaves the garden. She rushes off to find the disciples and spread the glorious news. Death did its worst but it couldn't hold onto Jesus. Mary has seen him. Their Lord has risen. Jesus is alive!

Teaching point

Jesus broke the power of death. He gives eternal life to all who love and follow him.

Bible base

John 20:1–18

Background information

When Jesus was travelling around with his disciples, he was supported by a group of women. Mary Magdalene was one of this group. Luke 8:2 tells us that Jesus had cured some of these women of evil spirits and diseases. It says that before Mary Magdalene met with Jesus, she was possessed by seven demons.

Songs

God's not dead (No)
How deep the Father's love
Risen!
We believe in God the Father

42. Comings, Goings and Coming Again
(The mountain's story)

A mountain, called the Mount of Olives, lies close to the city of Jerusalem. Like all mountains, it is really good at one thing. The mountain is good at being there. The trees, plants and grasses on its slopes all come and go. They grow up and then wither away. The people who dwell in the city come and go, too. They live for a time and then die. But the mountain stays put. And, in its own unspoken, mountainy way, it knows one thing – one thing that the people, with their great store of knowledge often miss. The mountain knows its Creator.

Imprinted on its matter is the memory of that time when the Lord of Creation spoke and everything came into being; sky, sea, trees, plants, animals and, of course, mountains – solid, fertile, carpeted with flowers – perfect mountains in a perfect world.

The thorns and thistles came later. They came when the people God put in charge of his world chose to go their own way. Then decay and death replaced the glory that kept

207

everything fresh and alive.

Now, though, there is a whole new chapter to the story. The Lord of Creation has spent 33 years upon earth. Like other humans, he's lived and died. But unlike anyone else, he's come back to life again. He's come back to life and today he's standing on the slopes of the mountain.

In its own silent, mountainy way, the mountain recognises its Maker. Like the rest of the created world, it knows who Jesus is. One word from him calmed a storm. One word from him withered a fig tree. One word from him and the mountain would cast itself into the sea. But Jesus isn't speaking to the mountain. He is speaking to his disciples, who have joined him on its slopes.

It's now 40 days since he rose from the dead. At different times and in different places, Jesus has appeared to these followers. Little by little, they're grasping the fact that the whole world has changed hands. The devil's reign of death is over and God's reign of new life has begun. It has begun in a hidden way in the hearts of believers like them, but soon it will be clear to everyone. Soon, Jesus will see to it that every trace of evil is wiped out and the earth is filled with his glory.

The big question is – when? When will this happen? That's what the disciples want to know. They're eager. They're impatient. And today, on the mountain slopes, they can hold back no longer. 'Lord,' they ask, 'Is this the time when you are going to take over?'

Instead of giving them an answer, Jesus gives them a job. He begins by explaining why he can't answer their question. The day when his full glory will be revealed will be decided by his heavenly Father. Right now, the important thing is that more and more people should get to know him. And this is where they, his followers, come in. For they are the ones who must tell everyone everywhere who he is and what he's done.

Everyone – gulp! – *everywhere*?

The disciples swallow hard.

Lovingly Jesus assures them they won't have to do it on their own.

'The Holy Spirit will come upon you and give you power,' he promises. 'Then you will tell everyone about me in Jerusalem, in all Judea, in Samaria and everywhere in the world.'

With these words, Jesus leaves the mountain. Most people leave a mountain by going down, but Jesus goes up. A white mist descends and, as it lifts, Jesus is lifted too... up... up... to vanish in the sky. Meanwhile, on the ground, his followers are joined by two angels. 'Jesus has been taken into heaven,' the angels say. 'But he'll come back as certainly as you have seen him go.'

Jesus will be back. Holding onto this promise, the disciples make their way to Jerusalem. But the mountain stays put. It is good at one thing – being there. It knows one thing – its Creator. And now, with the whole of the created world, it feels one thing – longing. In its own silent, mountainy way, the mountain groans with longing for that great day when the Lord of Creation will return. That day is getting closer. Soon – just as soon as the disciples' work is finished – Jesus will come again. There will be no more sickness or suffering or death. And on that day the mountain will sing.

Teaching point

One day, Jesus will come to judge the earth. In the meantime he gives Christians the job of telling others about him.

Bible base

Acts 1:6–12

Background information

The Mount of Olives is about 2,930 metres high. It is separated from Jerusalem by the Kidron valley. On one of its slopes, facing the Temple area of Jerusalem, there is the largest and oldest Jewish cemetery in the world. The Bible tells us that during his earthly ministry, it was Jesus' custom to go to the Mount of Olives in the evening (John 7:53 – 8:1), and tradition has made it the scene of his ascension. A prophecy in the book of Zechariah suggests that it may also be the scene of Christ's return (Zechariah 14:4).

Songs

And our voices will sing
Come on, let's get up and go
Go, go, go into all the world
Go, tell it on the mountain
God's raising up an army
Sing we of the King who is coming to reign
When the Lord in glory comes

Part Four

KINGDOM-BUILDING STORIES

True stories of faith in action

These stories are all based on the experiences of real children, although in some cases names and minor details have been changed. They are designed to encourage discussion and an active response, and should, ideally, be told in a setting which allows for this. Approximate age range varies – stories 43, 45, 48 and 49 should work with 6–10s; stories 44, 46, 47 and 50 are more suited to children aged 8+.

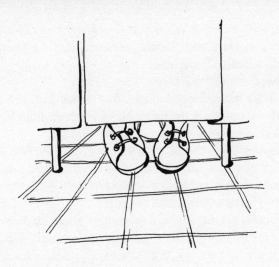

43. The Wee Ginger Boy
(Forgiving)

It was the first week of August and the Rea family were
enjoying the fun and fellowship of a Christian holiday camp
in Ireland. The Nesbitts – close friends from their church –
had come too. The families had put their tents up side by side,
and for the first few days five-year-old Jonathan Rea and the
eight-year-old Nesbitt twins were inseparable.

Then, one afternoon, as she relaxed with a mug of coffee,
Jonathan's mum, Carole, realised she hadn't seen her son
since lunch-time. She knew he was bound to be with the
twins, Gary and Stephen. Just to be on the safe side, though,
she decided to check.

'Jonathan!' she called.

There was no answer.

Carole Rea got to her feet and walked over to the Nesbitt's
tent. 'Jonathan, come out a minute, would you?'

But Jonathan didn't appear. Instead, there was a muffled
reply from inside the sleeping compartment. 'He isn't here.'

Not there? Sure enough, when Carole looked into the tent she saw that Gary and Stephen were playing on their own. 'Where's Jonathan?' she asked.

The twins shook their heads. 'Don't know.'

Mrs Rea's heart skipped a beat. She turned and spotted her husband coming along the path. 'Have you seen Jonathan?'

Jim Rea shook his head. 'He's with the Nesbitts.'

'No he isn't.' By now, Carole was worried. Jonathan wasn't the sort of boy to wander off on his own. So what could have happened to him? Had he lost himself in the woods. Or, worse still, could he have fallen into the lake?

For the next three-quarters of an hour the Reas toured the campsite, searching for their son. 'Have you seen a small boy with red hair?' they asked everyone they met. But nobody had. Back in the Nesbitt tent, meanwhile, the twins' mum had noticed something suspicious. There was a crack – a large crack – in the screen of the portable TV in the corner.

'Look! How on earth did that happen?' she wondered. 'It certainly wasn't broken this morning.'

Gary and Steve looked suitably puzzled and shocked.

'It must've been vandals!' muttered Gary.

'Bad boys from the village,' nodded Steve. 'They must've come in when we were out.'

'Yeah, we saw them earlier, hanging round the site,' Gary agreed.

Immediately, Mrs Nesbitt rushed off to tell Jonathan's parents what the twins had said. Could Jonathan have gone off with the village lads? As the families stood anxiously putting two and two together, a little girl arrived on the scene. 'If you're looking for a wee ginger boy, I saw him,' she piped up.

'Where? Where?' The adults were round her in an instant.

The child pointed across at the Nesbitt's tent. 'I saw him run from that tent into the toilets,' she said.

Of course, Jonathan's dad had already looked for Jonathan in the toilet block. It was one of the first places he'd checked. He hadn't been very thorough, though. So now Jim Rea went

back. 'Jonathan! Jonathan!' He went inside and walked along
the cubicles, calling Jonathan's name. What was that? He
paused. A small sound was coming from the end cubicle.
Sniff! Sniff! Sniff! 'Jonathan, is that you?' No answer – but
Jim spotted a familiar pair of five-year-old feet. With a cry of
relief, he pushed open the door and there was his red-headed
son, blinking up at him.

Jonathan had been in the toilets all along. He'd heard his
parents' calls, but he'd been too scared to come out. For he
was the one who'd broken the Nesbitt's TV. It had been an
accident, of course. He'd been playing with a mallet, flicking
the head off into the air, trying to act like Gary and Steve.
Then – crash! It had hit off the TV screen and Jonathan's
whole world had shattered with the glass. Leaving Steve and
Gary to dream up a story for their mum and dad, he'd bolted
off to hide in the toilets.

Now, though, everything was out in the open. Jim Rea took
the boy by the hand and led him back to the campsite, to the
tent where everyone was waiting – his mum, the twins, Mr and
Mrs Nesbitt. Wordlessly, the little boy looked around. This was
the moment – the horrible moment – he'd run away from.

But facing things turned out to be a lot easier than hiding.
Mr and Mrs Nesbitt didn't scold him for breaking the TV, and
Mr and Mrs Rea didn't scold Gary and Steve for covering up.

'I'll get the TV fixed,' Jim Rea said.

'Don't worry. It doesn't matter,' Harry Nesbitt grinned.

So, as swiftly as it had shattered, Jonathan's world came
back together. It was all right. He was forgiven. Everyone was
friends.

Still, the little incident left its mark, not on the TV, of
course – Jim Rea arranged with another friend in the church
to fix it for £5 – but on Jonathan, Gary and Steve. When accidents happen, own up – that was the lesson the three lads
learnt. And from then on if anything got mysteriously broken
or lost, Jonathan's dad would wink at Mum and say, 'It must
have been the wee ginger boy.'

Teaching point

We build God's kingdom when we build strong friendships with other Christians and forgive each other when we do wrong or make mistakes.

Bible base

Ephesians 4:25–32

Into action

Give the children a piece of paper and ask them to note down (or draw) anything they may have done that they feel ashamed of. Then burn the papers, or get the children to tear them up into tiny pieces. Explain that it is like this when mistakes and sins are forgiven – they are gone, wiped out.

God wants to forgive us when we do wrong. He also wants us to forgive others.

Songs

God loves you, and I love you
I was lost but Jesus found me
Our Father, who is in heaven
Think of a world without any flowers

44. A Truly Happy Christmas
(Praying and witnessing)

It was six o'clock on Christmas morning. David and Allen Campbell stood whispering loudly outside their parents' room. 'OK boys! We're awake. Let's go downstairs.' Their sleepy parents, Sam and Liz, hauled themselves out of bed.

Presents – that was always the first big excitement of Christmas Day. Once again, the downstairs lounge of the Campbell's home had turned into an Aladdin's cave overnight. 'Hey, look! We've got horses!' David squealed with delight at the sight of two large, brown rocking horses. 'And armour,' cried Allen. 'And a castle and a workman's bench. . . and annuals. . . and a football. . .'

'Happy Christmas, boys!' Their dad did his best to sound cheerful, but David noticed it was an effort. That hint of sadness reminded the boy that this couldn't really be a happy Christmas – not without Nana Campbell. Her death in the summer had left a great empty space in their lives. And, as if that wasn't bad enough, Papa Campbell was in hospital.

Later that morning, as usual, the Campbell family went to church. Going to church and following Jesus was something that was really important to them. 'Good Christian men, rejoice. . .' David sang loudly. His father sang too, trying to look on the bright side. At least Papa Campbell would be with them for dinner, even though the doctor had said he could only leave the ward for a few hours.

Back home, David and Allen waited eagerly for their grandfather.

'He's here! He's here!' They raced into the driveway to welcome the car. It was great to see Papa out of pyjamas and more like his normal self. He didn't say much, but that was expected. Nana had always done the talking. Papa was a quiet man. 'A real gentleman,' people used to say. He never spoke about his feelings but he was always very generous. That year, despite all his problems, he'd given the boys' aunt money to buy them a present. 'Wow! Thank you, Papa! Those are brilliant!' David gasped, tearing the paper off a big box of cars.

The family moved into the dining-room and sat down round the table. The boys' other granny and grandpa were with them, but Christmas dinner was still the hardest part of the day. Papa Campbell needed help to cut up his turkey and everybody really missed Nana's chat.

'All right, boys. You can go,' Dad said at last.

Hurrah! David and Allen shot off to their toys and the grown-ups went into the lounge. As they played, the boys could hear the chink of teacups and the quiet hum of voices. Outside, it began to get dark.

Papa will be leaving soon, David thought. With the thought came an idea. No, more than an idea – an inner push. It made the boy put his toy spanner back on the workman's bench and turn to his brother. 'Come on,' he said. 'I'm going into the lounge.' There was something he had to do – something he had to say – before Papa left the house.

So it came about that a few moments later, David did

something completely unexpected. He slipped into the lounge and went over to Papa Campbell's side. 'Papa,' he said simply. 'Don't you want to become a Christian? Then when you die you'll go to heaven and see Nana again?'

As he spoke, the cups stopped clinking and the whole room became still. The old man took his grandson's hand. He gripped it tightly and his blue eyes filled with tears. 'Yes,' he whispered. 'Yes, I want to become a Christian. I want that very much.'

Immediately, the family gathered round. They prayed for Papa and Papa prayed too, asking Jesus into his heart. Cue for a major hug-in! Papa hugged David. David hugged his dad, Sam. Sam hugged Papa. Everyone forgot about time. 'I suppose we'd better get over to the hospital,' Sam said in the end. Papa had already been out much longer than agreed. But he was looking so much better and in such good spirits the doctor surely wouldn't mind.

'Bye-bye, Papa. Happy Christmas!' David and Allen waved goodbye from the door.

As Papa Campbell waved back cheerfully, their dad marvelled again at what had taken place. Papa had joined God's family. This was something Sam had prayed for every single day for twelve years. He'd wanted to talk to his father about it. For all those years he'd been waiting for the right time to speak. And today David had spoken for him. He'd come in at exactly the right time and said exactly the right thing.

It was a truly happy Christmas after all.

Teaching point

We build God's kingdom when we pray for others to come to faith and look for the right opportunity to speak to them.

Bible base

Colossians 4:2–6

Into action

Spend a few moments praying with the children for family and friends. Explain that God often works in a hidden way in people's lives, giving them a desire to know him. Sometimes something as simple as an invitation to church can be just what they need to bring them into God's family. Encourage the children to invite others to their church group.

Songs

Colours of day dawn into the mind
If you want joy, real joy, wonderful joy
Prayer is like a telephone

45. *No Good at Sums*
(Healing)

Helen Lawrence liked almost everything about school. She liked her teacher and her classroom and break-time and games. The only thing Helen didn't like about school was work. Helen found schoolwork difficult – especially sums. No matter how hard she tried, she never seemed to be able to get her sums right. And spelling was a bit of a struggle too.

Helen started school in England, but when she was six her family moved to Africa. Helen's father was a doctor. The move meant he and Helen's mum could show God's love to those who were sick and help the people trying to bring healing.

Before long Helen had lots of friends in Africa. The girl wasn't at all shy, so making friends came easily to her. Of course, she knew not to speak to strangers if her mum and dad weren't around, but any time the family went visiting, she would chat away happily to everyone she met.

One evening, after school, Helen and her parents went to

visit a man called Joseph. They went to see him because he was ill and Dr Lawrence had heard he was lonely and depressed.

'Come in. . . you are very, very welcome,' Joseph's family greeted them warmly. Still, as the Lawrences sat down in the shady room, they felt uncomfortable. They noticed that the family didn't seem to have much to do with Joseph. The sick man was left to drink his tea alone on one side of the room, while everyone else sat on the other.

As Dr and Mrs Lawrence tried to think of ways of bringing Joseph into the conversation, Helen skipped across the room. To Helen, Joseph was another new friend waiting to be made.

She sat down in a seat beside him, eager to chat about some news she'd just heard.

'Dad told me you used to be a teacher,' she began.

'That is right,' Joseph nodded. 'Teaching was my job.'

'I go to school,' smiled Helen.

'And are you a good student?'

The girl shook her head. 'I try to be, but. . . the thing is. . . I'm hopeless at sums.'

'Hopeless at sums?' Joseph reached into his pocket and pulled out a pencil. 'If you like I will help you. We could do some sums now.'

This was a bit like offering someone who hated vegetables a plateful of Brussels sprouts. For a split second the girl hesitated. She flashed a quick look at her parents, who smiled encouragingly. Helen knew she could say 'no' to the sums, but it wouldn't be very friendly. 'All right, then,' she nodded. 'But don't make them hard.'

The girl needn't have worried. Doing adding and subtracting with Joseph wasn't a bit like school. He made it into a game. The time flew past, and all too soon her dad said they'd better be going.

'Goodbye, Joseph. I never knew sums could be such fun,' Helen said as she left. 'You're a great teacher.'

What neither the girl nor her parents knew at the time was

that the real teacher that afternoon had been Helen. It was only much later that they discovered how God had used her to speak to Joseph that day. 'You saw how Helen immediately accepted you. My love is like that. You don't have to earn it. Turn to me and I will accept you straight away, just as she did.' This was the message Joseph heard through Helen's chatter and smile. And, over the next few days, the young man opened his heart, and found the joy of being loved and accepted by God.

Joseph's family had also learnt a lesson that day. Until Helen came, they'd been keeping Joseph at a distance – afraid that if they touched him, he would infect them with his illness. But the sight of the girl at Joseph's side had shown them something. 'It's safe to be near Joseph.' That was the message they'd received. And from then on Joseph's family were ready to come close to him, too.

So the two hours that Helen spent in Joseph's house had a tremendous effect. Before her visit, Joseph was lonely and despairing. Afterwards, he felt accepted and full of joy. A mathematical genius could have stepped into his home and had no effect at all. But Helen transformed things – not by saying or doing anything brilliant; just by being her normal, friendly self.

Teaching point

We build God's kingdom when we bring his healing to those who are sick.

Bible base

Acts 9:32–35

Into action

Talk to the children about the different ways God heals people

– through medical treatment, through prayer and the laying on of hands (James 5:14,15), through rest and good food (1 Kings 19:3–9). Talk about the difference between spiritual and physical healing, and how God wants everyone to know his healing love.

Ask the children to think of people they know who are sick. Pray for these folk. If appropriate, arrange to visit them or send them a card from the group.

Songs

Jesus' hands were kind hands, doing good to all
Make me a channel of Your peace
Who took fish and bread, hungry people fed?

46. Rebecca's Wheelchair
(Caring)

Alex and Ben had two older sisters. Kim, their eldest sister, was grown up and lived close by. Rebecca, their second sister, lived with them at home. In lots of ways, Rebecca was more like a big baby sister than an older sister. She had beautiful blonde hair and wore the latest teenage fashions, but she couldn't talk to them or do much for herself. When they went out, she needed to be pushed in a wheelchair.

Because Rebecca was disabled, strangers sometimes acted as if she wasn't a proper person. Ben and Alex knew better. They knew that Rebecca enjoyed music and that red was her favourite colour. They knew that if she could have told them the thing she loved to do most, she would have said, 'I love to bounce.' When Rebecca bounced on a bed or a cushion, or even when the car went over a hump in the road, she laughed out loud. The doctor had explained this was because usually Rebecca didn't feel as if her legs belonged to her, but bouncing made her feel whole.

225

One November, when Alex was ten and Ben was twelve, the boys noticed that Rebecca didn't look comfortable in her wheelchair. She kept slipping down in it so that her bottom came half off the edge of the seat and her head and shoulders hung awkwardly over the side. They were really glad when they heard Mum saying Rebecca had an appointment at the wheelchair clinic.

Sure enough, Mum came back from the clinic with good news. Rebecca was to get a new wheelchair. 'It's brilliant – a completely different model,' Mum explained happily. 'The way it's moulded keeps her sitting nice and straight.'

The only problem was Rebecca couldn't get her wheelchair straight away. She'd have to wait for twelve weeks.

'She can't wait twelve weeks!' exclaimed Ben. 'She's uncomfortable. She needs it now.'

'I know,' sighed Mum. 'It's a real shame. The trouble is the wheelchair comes in a pack from abroad; then someone at the clinic has to put it together. We'll just have to be patient. . .'

Being patient wasn't easy – especially when taking Rebecca out for walks had become almost impossible. Every time she slipped down in her wheelchair, Alex and Ben counted the days until the beginning of February, when the twelve weeks would be up.

Finally, the day arrived. Excitedly, Mum rang the clinic. Oh dear! When she returned from the phone, her face was sad and her voice was flat. The wheelchair hadn't come.

It didn't come the next week either, nor the next week, nor the next.

'Please God, bless Rebecca. May she get her new wheelchair soon.' Night after night, Ben and Alex prayed the same prayer. Then, in March, something extraordinary happened. Rebecca managed to take a few steps without anyone holding her hands. 'Hey, look at you! Well done, Rebecca!' the boys marvelled. God was certainly blessing their sister. But her wheelchair still hadn't come.

Time went on. Winter turned to spring. The family began to

make summer holiday plans. Week after week, Mum rang the clinic, only to be told 'no wheelchair'.

In May Mum and Dad booked a holiday house for the first week of July. It was set in a magnificent 100-acre estate in the heart of the country. The plan was for Kim, Ben and Alex to do lots of cycling – and for Mum, Dad and Rebecca to go for lots of walks. It seemed like the ideal holiday – just as long as the new wheelchair arrived in time.

Now Ben and Alex were praying urgently: 'God, please let Rebecca get her wheelchair before the summer holidays. Please help people understand she really needs it.' Mum rang the clinic the first week in June, the second week in June, the third week in June. And then, the fourth week of June, a second extraordinary thing happened. Mum, who was always so patient, decided enough was enough. That week, when she heard the words 'no wheelchair', she didn't just put down the phone. 'You can expect my daughter and me at the clinic tomorrow,' she told the manager. 'And we won't leave the building without the wheelchair.'

'I'm ready to contact the TV and the papers,' Mum went on firmly. 'We'll stay at the clinic for as long as it takes.'

Well, this was a turn-up for the books. Ben and Alex tried to act normally as Mum prepared to leave with Rebecca next morning. It didn't feel like a normal trip to the clinic, though – more like a major expedition. They noticed her packing some chocolate.

'I suppose this means you mightn't be back for tea,' observed Ben.

'We'll be watching out for you on the six o'clock news,' joked Alex.

It didn't come to that. After nine months of waiting and praying, Mum and Rebecca drove home in triumph. At long last they had the new wheelchair in the boot of the car.

The wheelchair was back in the boot two days later, when the whole family set off on holiday. 'Thank you, God. Thank you for what you've done for Rebecca,' an unspoken prayer of thankfulness filled the car. Still, as they drove along the road, Alex had a question – something that had been on his mind for some time. 'Do you think,' he said, 'that if we prayed hard enough God would make Rebecca completely well?'

Mum and Dad exchanged glances. This was a question they'd struggled with themselves. 'I think God wants us to know that it's OK for Rebecca to be the way she is now,' Mum said softly. 'One day she'll walk and talk, but until then God has given us the job of loving her and fighting for her and working out what she wants. . .'

'Yeah, right,' interrupted Ben. 'So sink the boot, Dad. There's a hump in the road.'

'So there is!' Dad pressed down on the accelerator.

The car picked up speed. Up the side of the hump they zoomed and whoosh! Rebecca laughed out loud. Today, bouncing was what she wanted to do most – and her family would make sure that she bounced as high as she could.

Teaching point

We build God's kingdom when we help people with special needs live their lives to the full.

Bible base

1 Corinthians 12:12–14, 21–27

Into action

Talk with the children about people they know who are disabled. Encourage them to think of ways to get to know them better and find out what they enjoy. Plan an activity that will include them. Alternatively, involve a child who is disabled in planning an activity for the group.

Songs

Father God, I wonder
Go, tell it on the mountain
You're one in a million

47. One for Nan
(Encouraging)

There were times – and this was one of them – when Margaret wished she was more forgetful. Of course, the silver-haired old lady didn't want to start forgetting what day it was, or where she lived. What Margaret wished she could forget were her memories of the past. Yet here she was again, thinking of her childhood – and, as usual, her thoughts made her sad.

Margaret felt sad because soon after she was born her parents had lost their money. Being poor had made her father bitter, and her mother depressed. They'd seen to it that Margaret had food to eat and clothes to wear, but they hadn't been able to give the one thing she really wanted: a feeling of being loved.

'Things will be better when our ship comes in,' her mother used to sigh.

At the time, Margaret hadn't known this was just a saying. Day after day, she'd made her way to the docks. She'd stood there – a small, lonely figure beneath the cranes, looking out to sea, scanning the horizon for that special ship, the ship that

would solve all her problems, the ship full of fine clothes and
jewels that would mean she would never feel unloved again.

Of course, this ship hadn't come. Instead, Margaret had
grown up. She'd got married – had two children of her own –
worked hard, been happy. Still, there were times, like today,
when the unloved feeling flooded back.

The old lady shut her eyes. Perhaps a little doze would
cheer her up. But, instead, her dreams took her right back into
her childhood. There she was – a girl in a second-hand
pinafore with a thin, pinched face – helping her mother
unpack the groceries. Eagerly, she was lifting one purchase
after another from the bag . . . tea, sugar, half-a-dozen eggs.
'Mind now, Maggie,' her mother snapped. 'Those eggs cost
more than enough without you breaking them.'

The child bit her lip. She knew better than to answer back.
She clung on to her fading hope that Mother had bought her
some sweets from the shop – a couple of humbugs, a bar of
toffee. Longingly, she felt round the empty bag, exploring
every corner. No. Her shoulders drooped. There was nothing –
no wonderful surprise. As usual, Mother had bought nothing
but the groceries. The thought of buying sweets for her
daughter had never crossed her mind.

Drring . . . drring . . . drring. Three sharp rings of the doorbell brought Margaret back to the present. Drring . . . drring.
She opened her eyes. Someone was on the doorstep. Pulling
herself to her feet, the old lady glanced at the clock. My goodness! Was that the time? Her eyes brightened. School would
be over for the day. The caller might be her grandson.

And sure enough, no sooner had she opened the door than
nine-year-old Matthew bounded past her into the kitchen,
where he dumped his school bag on the floor. 'You'll never
guess what we did in class, Nan,' he beamed. 'Cookery!'

He unzipped the bag, burrowed inside and pulled out a
plastic container. 'We made flapjacks,' he went on. 'And Miss
White said we could bring one home for each member of our
family. I told her I needed three – one for Mum, one for Dad

and one for my Nan. So here you are. You can have it for your afternoon tea.' Proudly, he handed over a large, crumbly flap-jack, generously sprinkled with sugar.

'Why, Matthew!' Margaret gasped. 'What a wonderful sur-prise!'

And truly it was as if the sun had come out. Suddenly, instead of regretting the past, Margaret saw the good things God had done in her life. She might not have got sweets from her mother, but her grandson had brought her this treat. She was part of a loving family. 'One for Mum, one for Dad and one for my Nan,' Matthew had said. It was like being given the crown jewels, knowing that she was special to him.

'Take a bite, Nan. Go on,' the boy urged.

Briefly, Margaret hesitated. The flapjack meant so much, really she would have preferred to frame it. But the boy was hopping eagerly from foot to foot, blue eyes dancing with impatience.

So Margaret bit into the glistening biscuit, only to get a sec-ond surprise. Her grandson made first-class biscuits! 'Mmmm lovely . . . it's delicious,' she smiled, as the flapjack melted in her mouth.

Teaching point

We build God's kingdom when we comfort and encourage others by things we say and do.

Bible base

2 Corinthians 7:5–7

Into action

Encourage the children to pray for their grandparents and for older members of the church family. Discuss things they can say and do to remind them they are loved and special.

Songs

Crunch, crunch, crunch
God gave me ears
I'm special because God has loved me
One, two, three, Jesus loves me

48. Lali and Moni
(Using gifts and abilities)

Lali Sakar and her friend Moni Hari grew up in one of the most crowded places on earth. The Calcutta slum, where they lived, was crammed full of noise, smells, ragged people, hunger, sickness and despair. Still, the girls felt lucky. They didn't have much food or education. But at least they had roofs over their heads and their parents cared for them as best they could. Lali and Moni knew lots of children who weren't so fortunate. Many had parents addicted to drugs or alcohol. Others lived alone on the street, scavenging for scraps in the rubbish.

When they were small, Lali and Moni didn't think much about these problems. They'd never known anything different. Then, one day, a lady from a Christian organisation came to their area. She talked to all the parents about a children's club that had started nearby. 'We run it every morning,' she explained. 'There are games and activities. We'd be glad if you'd let your children come along.'

234

Lali and Moni were excited to hear about the club. They were even more excited next morning, when their parents said they could go.

That morning, life started to change for Lali and Moni. The club, they discovered, was like a really relaxed school. There were lessons, food, fun, friends. Needless to say, the girls went back the next day – and the next day... and the next...

Years passed, and Lali and Moni kept attending the club. They learnt to take pride in their homes and in their appearance; they also learnt how to read and write. Two of the activities they enjoyed most were dancing and singing. One song they sometimes sang began, 'Jesus' love is bubbling over.' Those words described the feeling the girls had whenever they came to the club. It was a place where love and happiness bubbled over into their lives.

Outside though, life was very different. The older the girls got, the more they noticed things that were wrong in the slum. But how could they change things for the better? They were still young – just into their teens. And then they discovered there was a way for them to make a difference – a way most girls their age would never think of.

Lali and Moni could see how lots of women in the slum were held back by not being able to read or write. Reading and writing was like a key that unlocked all sorts of doors. People who could read and write felt better about themselves and had more opportunities than people who couldn't. So, when a special teacher came to the club centre and offered to train the girls to teach adults, Lali and Moni jumped at the chance.

The girls were six years younger than most trainee teachers. Still, they completed the course with flying colours. They were ready to start teaching. But would they have any pupils? And if they did get pupils, would those pupils manage to learn?

It turned out that the answer was 'yes' to both questions. By the time Lali was fourteen and Moni was fifteen they had their own class of twenty mothers. First, the women learnt to hold their pencils correctly; then they learnt how to make strokes on the page – and before long they were writing their own names. For Lali and Moni this was always a great moment – when a woman wrote her own name for the first time, then looked up, her eyes full of pride.

Not long after Lali and Moni started their classes, a visitor came to the classroom. His name was Tim, and he worked for an organisation that supported this work. He'd come all the way from England to find out more about it. The minute he heard what Lali and Moni were doing, he wanted to interview them.

'Do you mind talking to me about yourselves?' he asked them, through an interpreter.

'We don't mind,' the girls agreed. Once they would have been too shy to speak to visitors, but thanks to the club, they weren't afraid now. So they told Tim all about their pupils, about their ambition to become qualified teachers and about their families and homes. Tim was really impressed. He told them about Christians in his country who gave money and prayed for their work.

'What would you ask them to pray for?' was one of the things he wanted to know.

'Ask them to pray that we will study well and be able to carry on what we are doing,' began Lali.

'And that we can help others the way we have been helped,' Moni added, with a smile.

Teaching point

We build God's kingdom when we use our gifts to help those around us.

Bible base

Romans 12:3–8

Into action

Help the children to recognise some gifts God has given them. Can they think of ways to use them that will make life better for others?

The community centre where Lali and Moni teach is run by Emmanuel Ministries, Calcutta, and is supported by Tearfund. A gift to help with work of this kind could be sent to Tearfund, 100 Church Road, Teddington, Middlesex TW11 8QE.

Songs

Corinthians' gifts
Crunch, crunch, crunch
We really want to thank You Lord

49. The Street Sale
(Fundraising)

Eight-year-old Michelle Callan wanted to raise money. Michelle didn't want money for herself. She wanted it to help people in other countries – people who were victims of famine and disaster. Michelle had already raised £10 selling toys and pictures to visiting relatives. Now she felt ready to try something bigger.

'Remember how I sold some of my toys and pictures last year and gave away the money?' she said to her parents. 'Well, I think I could raise a lot more money if I set up a stall outside the front gate.'

A stall outside the front gate?! Michelle's parents looked uneasy. They certainly weren't against the idea of raising money to help people. But a street sale was very public. None of the other children in the leafy housing estate where they lived had ever done such a thing.

Once she'd shared her idea, Michelle wasn't prepared to forget it. 'Please can I have a street sale,' she would plead,

238

any time she heard news of famines or disasters.

'All right, you can have a street sale,' her parents agreed in the end. 'But not tomorrow, or even next week. You can have it in October.'

October was three months away. The idea behind the wait was to give Michelle time either to change her mind or to get organised. No prizes for guessing which the girl did. She began by sharing the plan with the Keegan sisters, who lived across the road, and with her friend Megan Grant, who lived next door.

'I'm holding a street sale in October. Will you help me?' she asked.

'Yes, that's a great idea,' Grace, Avril and Megan agreed.

The next step was gathering up things to sell. Michelle got in touch with her cousins and asked them for any cuddly toys they no longer wanted; she went round some of the neighbours' houses and collected old ornaments and bits of bric-a-brac. The girls washed the cuddly toys, cleaned the ornaments, and Michelle got her dad to fix things that were broken – like the wooden book-ends given by Mrs Quirk. One way and another, by the time October came, they had lots of things for the stall.

The day before the sale every item had to be priced. Michelle knew that most of the customers were likely to be children, so she kept the prices low. 'We mustn't charge more than fifty pence for anything,' she told her friends. She also knew that people needed to know what the sale was in aid of, so the girls painted two big posters with the words SALE FOR THE POOR IN AFRICA printed in bright blue, green and yellow letters.

Those posters fluttered in the breeze as Mr Callan helped Michelle carry the table out to the front gate next morning. The sale was due to start at midday. Michelle had worked out that four helpers might not be enough to cope with all the customers, so she'd asked a friend from church to help too. Carolyn arrived promptly at a quarter to twelve, but there was no sign of Avril, Megan or Grace. What had happened to them? Michelle skipped across the road to inquire.

Her friends opened the door, looking unhappy. 'I'm really sorry,' Avril muttered. 'We're not allowed out.'

Neither, it turned out, was Megan. This was a big blow. In one stroke, Michelle had lost three assistants. 'I'll stay and help if you like,' her dad offered. But the girl shook her head. The sale wouldn't be the same if her mum or dad helped. It was something she had to handle herself.

Twelve o'clock came. The stall was officially open. Five minutes. . . twenty. . . twenty-five minutes passed, and nobody came. Not a single customer. After thirty minutes Michelle's dad, watching from an upstairs window, could stand it no longer. Unknown to Michelle, he picked up the phone and tipped off a friendly neighbour. 'Hello, Joe, this is Brian. Look, would you and the family take a stroll down to our gate?'

Maybe it was as a result of this phone call, but the next time Mr Callan glanced out of the window, business was booming. A cluster of parents and children had gathered round the table, clearly delighted with what they found.

Next thing, Grace, Avril and Megan appeared on the scene. 'It's all right. We can help, after all!' Avril beamed. Happily, the friends joined Michelle and Carolyn, just in time to sell Mrs Quirk's son, Jack, a fine pair of book-ends. (Yes, Mrs Quirk had given them and Jack had bought them back!) Jack was just one of many satisfied customers to walk off with a bargain that afternoon. Money changed hands so rapidly that by four o'clock the table was practically bare. The Keegan sisters kept things going a little longer, running home and finding extra toys to sell; but finally, at five o'clock, Michelle called it a day. With no more customers and an empty stall, all that remained to be done was count the takings.

How much had they raised? That was the big question. Eagerly, the girls tipped out their cash box – and counted £56. While they were squealing with excitement, there was a ring of the doorbell. A neighbour, who had missed the sale, wanted to donate £5.

The grand total of £61 was more than anyone had expected. 'A superb effort. Well done!' That was what Michelle's minister said, when he was presented with the money. A few days later the group received an official 'thank you' letter, promising the Missionary Society would put their gift to good use.

'There now! Isn't that nice. We must keep the letter safe,' Mr and Mrs Callan said, proudly.

And, of course, Michelle kept the letter. It was good to know their efforts were appreciated. It was even better to know that she and her friends had really helped people in need. But the street sale was over – and the needs were still there. Already she was asking, 'What next?'

Teaching point

We often hear about victims of famine and disaster. We build God's kingdom when we do something to help them.

Bible base

James 2:14–17

Into action

Show the children a map of the world. Point out a country which has recently been hit by natural disaster. Talk about what happened and the needs of the people who live there. Encourage the children to think how they could raise money to help them.

Songs

Go, tell it on the mountain
I'm working out what it means to follow Jesus
Jesus' hands were kind hands

50. Lighter and Brighter
(Sharing in work and worship)

Kirsty, Bethany and Rebekah belonged to a Pathfinders group. The eleven girls and lads got together every Sunday morning in a room in Christchurch, their local church. Most weeks, the three friends enjoyed these meetings. They liked Rachel, Hannah and Ann, their leaders, and they had some good discussions about God. Now and again, though, the sessions felt a bit flat – like coke with the fizz gone out of it. The room where they met didn't help. Somehow, even in the middle of summer, it felt cool. Its magnolia walls, beige ceiling and plain brown carpet were as dull as an overcast sky.

One Sunday, when the girls came into the building, they noticed an unusual smell – a sharp, fresh, straight-to-the-sinuses sort of smell. Kirsty wrinkled her nose.

'Paint.' Rebekah pointed at some paint tins in the corner. 'The Youth Fellowship have been decorating. I heard Rachel say they were doing up their room.'

The girls went on upstairs into their own room, which today

reminded Bethany of cold mushroom soup. 'This place needs doing up, too,' she whispered. Rebekah looked round. There wasn't much wrong with the room. Adults might even describe it as tasteful. But it was a taste with no flavour – like crisps without salt. 'Yeah, something needs to be done,' she agreed.

One of the things the girls liked about their leaders was their openness to suggestions. But nothing had quite prepared them for the reaction when they suggested the Pathfinders' room needed a coat of paint. It was like putting a match to brushwood. No sooner had Rachel mentioned it to the rest of the group than – whoosh! – the idea caught fire. Yes, the place definitely needed painting, everyone insisted, but not the same colours as before. It should have a new colour-scheme – something lighter and brighter, something they'd chosen themselves – and yes, why not (by now everyone was really excited), they could paint the room themselves, too.

Or could they? Rachel didn't want to be a wet blanket, but she spotted one rather large hurdle ahead. The Pathfinders' room was church property. 'That means we need permission before we can change anything,' she warned.

Now, if you were to ask, what sort of creatures do church property committees resemble, the answer would be owls. Owls are wise but wary. Leaders responsible for church property are, too. So there was quite a bit of nervous blinking when the Christchurch leaders were asked to let the Pathfinders repaint their magnolia walls. Wisely, though, they said: 'Yes.' The warier ones could be heard adding things like, 'It's a bit of a risk,' and, 'I hope there'll be adults involved.' Still, they didn't screech and peck the idea to death, and that was the main thing.

Now that the Pathfinders had the go-ahead, they didn't waste any time. Sunday found them poring over dozens of strips of paint on cards, deciding on a colour scheme.

'How about black for the walls, purple for the doors and orange for the skirting-boards?' someone joked.

'No way. The warden would have a heart attack.'

'I like this colour.' Bethany pointed to a lilac strip. 'With this.' Kirsty pointed to a green one.

The combination drew nods of agreement. It was different, without being over the top.

So the leaders went out and bought six cans of lilac paint and four cans of green.

A few days later, armed with paintbrushes, Bethany, Kirsty, Rebekah and the other Pathfinders made their way to the church. There, they found the floor of their room had already been swathed in sheets – ready for work to begin.

'This is scary!' Rebekah muttered, as she dipped her brush in the paint.

'I know. What if we make a mess of it?' Bethany painted a long, lilac streak down the wall.

The girls needn't have worried. Before long, the whole group were wielding their brushes like professionals. They discovered exactly how much paint they could pick up without dripping. They learnt how to apply it to the walls smoothly so the brush strokes didn't show. Swish. . . swish. . . swish. . . swish. . . the rhythmic work loosened tongues. Patch by patch, the walls of the Pathfinders' room changed hue, and the group found themselves talking about anything and everything – home, school, God – until, all too soon, the transformation was complete.

The following Sunday, the Pathfinders met for the first time in their newly decorated room. Once it had been the colour of a dentist's surgery. Now it was more like a forest in spring. 'A fantastic job! Well done!' One of the church leaders poked his head round the door. Before long it became clear that this was more than a surface change. As the children pulled their chairs round into a circle for their usual time of Bible discussion and prayer, the leaders noticed the difference. The group was sharing more freely and openly than ever before. Working together had brought them all closer. There was a new lightness and brightness in their relationship – a new joy in learning together about God.

Teaching point

We build God's kingdom when we share together in work and worship.

Bible base

Hebrews 10:23–25

Into action

Write the headings **The Best Things** and **The Worst Things** on two sheets of paper. Talk with the children about the things they like most about being together and note them on the first sheet. Make a note on the second sheet of the things they like least. Write the heading **Action Plan** on a third sheet. Discuss what could be done to make the group even better, and plan to do it.

Songs

For I'm building a people of power
God loves you, and I love you
Peace is flowing like a river
We really want to thank You, Lord

Subject Index

Numbers refer to stories not page numbers

Abilities 45, 48
Accidents 43
Advice 25
Agents, secret 9
Angels 29
Animals, cruelty to 27
Anna 30
Appearances 19, 38

Babies 13
Baptism of Jesus 31
Battles 17, 25
Birth of Jesus 29, 30
Birthdays 13
Bread 21
Building 28
Bullies 25

Cakes 17
Calcutta 48
Camping 43
Caring for the sick 45
Centurions 40
Change 10
Choices 28, 33

Christmas 27, 29, 44
Church life 50
Computers 11
Consideration 16
Contentment 11
Conversion 36, 44
Cookery 47
Creation 5
Crucifixion 40
Cruelty to animals 27

Death 44
Decisions 2
Decorating 50
Demons 19

Eggs 20
Encouragement 47
Entertaining 34
Excuses 20

Failure 26
Fairness 21
Faith 19, 35
Farmers 20

Fear 3
Fishing 33
Following Jesus 33
Forgiveness 43
Friends 18, 49

Generosity 22
Gifts 45, 48
Giving 38
God
  His will 12
  Promises 30
  Putting him first 2, 14
Gossip 23
Grandparents 44, 47
Growth, spiritual 13
Guidance 1

Headmasters 24
Healing 35
Heaven 29
Helping others 18
Hens 20
Holidays 46
Holy Spirit 42
Horses 22

Idols 3

Jairus 35
Jealousy 11
Jesus
  Arrest 39
  Ascension............................ 42
  Baptism of 31
  Betrayal 39
  Birth 29, 30
  Death 40
  Following him 33
John the Baptist 31
Judas 39
Judges 21
Jumble sales 10

King Alfred 17

Laziness 20

Leadership 1
Lies 10
Life, sanctity of 7
Listening 24
Little Red Riding Hood 15

Marriage 8
Martha (and Mary) 34
Mary Magdalene 41
Mary the Mother of Jesus 32
Meals 34
Memories 47
Miracles 32
Money 21, 49
Mothers 16
Mount of Olives 42
Murder 7

Names 4
Needs 22, 49

Organising 49
Owning up 43

Parents 6, 37
Peer pressure 15
Peter 33
Pets 6, 27
Pharisees 31, 37
Pigs 28
Power 39
Prayer 25, 44, 46
Priorities 34
Promises of God 30

Questions 41

Reading 48
Red Riding Hood 15
Relationships 12
Rescue 9
Respect 6
Rest 5
Resurrection 41
Rewards 12
Risk 9
Rules 37

Sabbath 5
Sales 49
Salvation 40
Sanctity of life 7
School 24
Schoolwork 45
Secret agents 9
Secrets 23
Self-control 17
Selfishness 18
Sharing 50
Simon Peter 33
Sin 31, 40
Slums 48
Snow White 16
Special needs, people with 46
Spiritual growth 13
Spiritual healing 45
Stealing 9
Sunday 5
Superstition 3
Swearing 4
Synagogue 35

Tax collectors 36
Teaching 48
Telling others 42
Temple 30, 38
Tongue 23
Toys 26
Turning-points 26

Unpopularity 36

Violence 7

Wealth 38
Weddings 32
Wheelchairs 46
Widows 38
Will of God 12
Wisdom 14
Witness 44
Worry 19
Writing 48

Zacchaeus 36

Scripture Index

Numbers refer to stories not page numbers

Exodus
20:1–3 2
20:1–17 .... 1, 12
20:4,5 3
20:7 4
20:8–11 5
20:12 6
20:13 7
20:14 8
20:15 9
20:16 10
20:17 11

Deuteronomy
6:1–9 13

2 Chronicles
1:7–12 14

Proverbs
1:10 15
3:28 18
9:10 14
11:13 23
11:25 22

12:10 27
12:16 17
12:25 19
14:11 28
18:13 24
20:18 25
21:3 21
22:13 20
24:16 26
27:14 16

Isaiah
53:1–6 40

Matthew
3 31
21:1–11 39
26:1–55 39
27:32–54 40

Mark
5:21–43 35
7:1–13 37

Luke
2:8–14 29
2:21–38 30
5:1–11 33
10:38–42 34
19:1–9 36
21:1–4 38

John
2:1–11 32
20:1–18 41

Acts
1:6–12 42
9:32–35 45

Romans
12:3–8 48

1 Corinthians
12:12–14 46
12:21–27 46

2 Corinthians
7:5–7 47

Ephesians
   4:25–32 43

Colossians
   4:2–6 44

Hebrews
   10:23–25 50

James
   2:14–17 49

Children's Ministry Teaching Programme

- Do you want to see children develop a personal relationship with Jesus?

- Do you want teaching sessions that are fun, biblical, evangelical and interactive?

- Would you like children to enjoy age-appropriate activities as they learn about God?

If you've said YES to any of these questions, you need the Children's Ministry Teaching Programme.

The Children's Ministry Teaching Programme provides four leader's guides covering ages from under 3 to 13+; KidZone activity books for children aged 5-7, 7-9 and 9-11; MiniKidz and KidZone craft books for children aged 3-5 and 5-9, a magazine for those over 11; a CD of music and stories; and FamilyZone with song words, ideas for all-age worship and parents' letters.

For more information visit our web site
www.childrensministry.co.uk

50 Five-Minute Stories

by Lynda Neilands

'Please tell us a story...'

When you want something to fill the next five or ten minutes, something that will hold the children's attention and stay in their minds, this book will provide the fresh ideas and once-upon-a-time stories you need.

LYNDA NEILANDS is the author of the Brownie Guide Handbook as well as several children's novels. She lives in Belfast with her husband and twin sons – who have road-tested these stories.

50 Stories for Special Occasions

by Lynda Neilands

Good stories teach values, touch the emotions, foster empathy, lodge in the memory and can be a powerful vehicle for spiritual truth.

This is a book of stories for telling to children. Divided into sections, one for each month of the year, here you will find stories appropriate for:

- Christmas
- Easter, Harvest
- Valentine's Day
- Mothering Sunday
- Bible Sunday
- Father's Day

...and many more!

Each story is accompanied by an application, teaching point, Bible reading and a list of relevant songs.

CHILDREN'S
MINISTRY